Landing Force

48

Landing Force

48

FRANK V. GARDNER

To order additional copies of this book, contact:
Xlibris Corporation
1-888-795-4274
www.Xlibris.com
Orders@Xlibris.com
80904

CONTENTS

ILLUSTRATIONS

Cover Photo: The original flag raising on Mount Suribachi, Iwo Jima. Taken by Sgt. Lou Lowery USMC, a photographer for Leatherneck magazine.

POEMS

*   *   *

ACKNOWLEDGEMENTS

I could not have written this book without the support and encouragement of my wife, Gerry, and my daughter, Rosemarie. I thank both of them for the help they provided and the patience with me they displayed during this effort.

Rosemarie's computer equipment, training, and technical advice were invaluable. For these, I am especially grateful.

I also want to thank my son Tommy, a fellow Marine and my daughter Lorraine. In 2010 they helped a great deal regarding the publishing efforts of this book.

Proofreading and editing were graciously provided after Frank's death by his daughter, Diane, before the book went to print.

AUTHOR'S NOTE

"What did you do in the war, daddy?" That was a question many World War II veterans answered from time to time. When my children were small, I had told them a few old war stories; but I spared their tender ears from hearing unpleasant details about the war.

One day in 1994, when I was recalling aloud a vivid battle scene, my daughter, Ellen, remarked that she didn't realize I had been so involved with combat action on the Pacific islands.

I reflected back fifty years, when I served as a Marine sergeant and radio operator during World War II. Forty-seven men and I fought in the three toughest island battles of the Central Pacific. It's a distinction not matched by any other unit. We 48 Marines were unique also by virtue of our involvement in the three elements of air, land, and sea. In training, we were "air transportable." In combat, we provided air warning and later, close air support. Nine different Navy ships transported us some twenty thousand miles back and forth across the open seas of the wide Pacific Ocean. En route, we landed on three crucial islands where we fought a fanatical enemy and survived those historic battles. I realized that I did have a story to tell my family, not only about the war, its history, and the fighting, but also to record some personal experiences not necessarily associated with combat activity.

Significant portions of my story are in the form of letters I sent home during the war, 164 of them saved by my mother, Marie B. Gardner, and my two sisters, Dorothy and Mary. For these I am most grateful. I have printed appropriate excerpts of them throughout the book. Also, in 1998,

I upgraded the 1995 version, adding 100 related photographs and maps to better tell the story.

I survived those three horrendous battles and came home to live, work, and raise my family in this free country. I therefore dedicate this book to my wife, Gerry, and to our nine children, Karen, Diane, Maureen, Lorraine, Daniel, Rosemarie, Ellen, Nancy, and Thomas.

Also, I dedicate my efforts to the memory of those who did not come home, the 23,000 American men of the Army (5,529), Navy (5,800), and Marines (11,838), who died fighting for those three small islands with strange sounding names.

My story is about a time when Marine divisions landed and fought their way across the Central Pacific Ocean in eight major island battles. In the three toughest of those amphibious operations, each of the six Marine divisions became fully involved, either on Saipan, Iwo Jima, or Okinawa.

I landed with them on those three islands, providing technical assistance and close air support for each of the six Marine divisions of World War II.

FVG

PART ONE

*Marine Corps Training in
Five States*

CHAPTER 1

* * *

Remember Pearl Harbor

On December 7, 1941, a football game was played in the Nation's Capital on a Sunday afternoon. The next day's game report in the New York Times was datelined Washington, December 7. The first paragraph read, "Slingin' Sammy Baugh rifled three touchdown passes to give the Washington Redskins a 20-14 victory over the Philadelphia Eagles in a National League Football game."

As I was listening to the radio broadcast during the Sunday game, I could hear the public address system in the background. The announcer at the old Griffith Stadium on Georgia Avenue was paging one high-ranking military officer after another, generals and admirals alike, who were in attendance. They were being told to call or report to their offices. There was a stir among the fans watching the game. The people in the stadium knew something momentous must have happened.

Later that Sunday afternoon the entire American public learned what it was. The Japanese had bombed Pearl Harbor! I did not know where Pearl Harbor was, and neither did most Americans. That ignorance quickly changed, as did all of our lives.

We learned that Pearl Harbor, located in the Hawaiian Islands, was our greatest naval base in the Pacific Ocean. Our armed forces on the island of Oahu, principally the Navy, had suffered an unprovoked, sneak attack by the Japanese. Casualties were heavy and some of our ships were sunk in the harbor.

The next day, Monday, December 8, 1941, President Franklin D. Roosevelt addressed an emergency joint session of Congress. He opened his remarks by stating: "Yesterday, December 7, 1941, a date which will live in infamy, the United States of America was suddenly and deliberately attacked by naval and air forces of the Empire of Japan." He went on to ask Congress to declare war on Japan.

I, along with classmates and faculty members at Mount Saint Mary's College, listened by radio. That short but moving speech, broadcast nationwide, may have been the most memorable radio address in American history up to that time. Congress then formally declared war within the hour. This would be called the Second World War or World War II.

The New York Times of December 9 stated that the first reports of casualties counted 1,500 Americans killed and a like number wounded. One battleship and one destroyer were reported sunk, and other ships damaged.

Shortly after the Japanese attack, a new song was introduced, played, and sung over the radio. We all got to know it in those early months of the war:

> **Let's remember Pearl Harbor, as we go to meet the foe.**
> **Let's remember Pearl Harbor, as we did the Alamo.**
> **We will always remember how they died for liberty.**
> **Let's remember Pearl Harbor, and go on to victory!**

Since the Japanese were aligned with the other two Axis powers, Germany and Italy, we soon found our nation at war with those two European countries, as well.

Years later we would learn from the full report on Pearl Harbor that 3,077 Americans had been killed, and 1,355 wounded. The casualties included sixty-eight civilians. Four of our battleships were sunk and three were badly damaged. Eleven other American warships were sunk or badly damaged. Almost 200 of our airplanes had been destroyed on the ground. Fortunately, our four large aircraft carriers were not in the harbor, but were out of the area, on maneuvers at the time.

Of the 432 Japanese carrier planes that participated in the raid on Pearl Harbor, twenty-nine were shot down, accounting for fifty-five enemy fliers killed. Also, nine crewmen were killed from a few Japanese midget submarines that tried to sneak into the harbor the same day. A count of the enemy wounded that day was never established.

Fifty-three years later, on November 21, 1994, the Japanese Foreign Ministry apologized for not having warned that Japan was at war with the United States before attacking Pearl Harbor. According to the Associated Press, documents declassified in Tokyo in November 1994 said that the ministry had blundered in 1941 by not warning Japan's embassy in Washington that it needed to communicate the declaration of war urgently. "It is extremely regrettable" that such an inexcusable thing happened, said ministry spokesman Terusuke Terada.

In 1942, I was a sophomore at Mount Saint Mary's College in Emmitsburg, Maryland, performing part-time work on campus under the National Youth Administration to help with my tuition. In March of that year, I took a Red Cross training course at our college indoor swimming pool and was certified as a water-safety instructor. Meanwhile, as meat and sugar became rationed, I signed up for my share of food stamps back home. Also, being in the young men's category, ages 18 to about 30, I registered for the Selective Service draft in Washington.

During the summer of 1942, as a Red Cross Water-Safety Instructor, I conducted swimming classes and worked as a lifeguard at McKinley Swimming Pool in Northeast Washington. I rented a small room at the home of Mrs. Meyers, 22 T Street, Northwest, so that I could walk the three or four blocks to the pool. I put together a swimming team of youngsters who competed in the citywide tournament and won the championship at the end of the summer.

Twice a month that summer, I received two pay checks: a larger amount from the city's Welfare and Recreation Association for my work as a lifeguard; and a smaller amount from the Playground Department for teaching swimming. On July 21, the amounts were $38.75 and $26.00, respectively.

I kept a notebook of my expenditures. Selected entries are, as follows:

August 14, 1942		*August 27, 1942*	
Weighed: 150 pounds		Rent for the week	5.00
Breakfast	.30	Breakfast	.27
Lunch	.35	Lunch	.27
Snack	.24	Dinner	.80
Supper	.30	Phone call	.05
Treat Dorothy and Mary	.65	Coke	.05
Shoe shine	.25		

Following are some other expenditures that I recorded:

7/25 - New pair pants	2.45	8/8 - Clothes pins	.10
7/26 - Laundry	2.57	8/19 - Treat swim team	1.78
7/31 - Bought book, "You Are What	.98	8/23 - Sunday collection	.25
You Eat," by Victor H. Lindlahr		8/24 - Swim trunks	1.00
8/5 - Doctor for earache	1.00	8/28 - Laundry	.26
8/6 - Sent home	10.00	8/29 - Soap and toothbrush	.45
8/7 - Medicine for ears	.50	9/13 - Weekly transit pass	1.25
8/7 - Fountain pen (Parker)	3.00	9/22 - Two Redskin tickets	2.20
8/8 - Haircut	.80	9/23 - Half soles & heels	1.60

In those early months of 1942, the war had not been going well for the United States. We had already lost the Philippines, Guam, and Wake Island to the Japanese. So I decided that at the end of the summer, I would not go back to college, but would enlist in the Armed Forces and get into the fighting. This would mean not returning to my third year of college, where the Mount was embarking on a Navy V-12 officer-training program. My mother, however, had already refused to sign parental consent for my entry into that program.

On August 7, 1942, the First Marine Division landed on a place none of us had ever heard of: Guadalcanal, an island in the South Pacific. With little opposition at first, the Marines wrested a small airfield from the Japanese. Over the next two months, however, the Japanese poured heavy reinforcements onto the large island, attempting to recapture the airfield; but our forces held onto their small beachhead against overwhelming odds.

Guadalcanal was the first offensive land action taken against either of our main enemies, Japan or Germany, during World War II. The reports of the valiant efforts of those beleaguered fighting men against the enemy stirred my blood. I began to think of joining the Marines.

When the swimming pool closed at the end of the summer, I decided not to return to college, since I was planning to enlist. First, I went back to work at one of my old jobs on the soda fountain and lunch counter of Shepherd Park Pharmacy at the northern end of Georgia Avenue in Washington. I worked there only for the week of September 14 to 18, and was paid $13.86.

Before enlisting, I wanted to see my beloved Washington Redskins one last time. I went to Griffith Stadium and paid $1.10 to watch the game from the bleacher seats. The New York Times of September 21, 1942, reported:

> Washington—September 20. Young Steve Juzwick, a first-year recruit from Notre Dame, and the veteran Sammy Baugh sparked the Washington Redskins to a 28-14 victory over the Pittsburgh Steelers in a National Football League game before 25,000 fans today.
>
> . . . Baugh, as usual was in a class by himself in the passing department . . . .
>
> . . . In the fourth quarter . . . a quick kick by Baugh put the Steelers in a hole. Sammy then intercepted Tomasic's long pass on the Pittsburgh 29, raced to the 3, and from there rifled a toss to Ed Justice for the final score.

On September 23, I tried another job, working as an accounting clerk for the British Purchasing Commission in the 1400 Block of K Street, Northwest. After a few days at that desk job, I resolved to do something more important for the war effort. I decided to enlist in the Marines without any further delay.

CHAPTER 2

* * *

Boot Camp at Parris Island, South Carolina

I enlisted in the Marines on September 30, 1942, and was given serial number 481357. The next day, I said good-bye to my mother and my sisters. I boarded a train at Union Station in Washington. At Yemassee, South Carolina, I, along with about fifty recruits, left the train. I remember handing my jacket and necktie to the old Negro porter as he bade good-bye to us at the station. I said, "Here, I won't be needing these for a while." Then we made the thirty-mile truck ride to the Marine Corps Recruit Depot at Parris Island, South Carolina.

At boot camp we shed our civilian clothing and our hair, put on olive-green dungarees, and began doing close-order drill with Springfield 1903 rifles.

During the next three years of the war I wrote almost two hundred letters home, 164 of which were saved by my mother and my two sisters, Dorothy and Mary. In this book, I have interspersed many of those letters or excerpts thereof. They depict my training, traveling, experiences in the Pacific, and the conduct of the war as I came to appreciate it.

I wrote several letters home from boot camp. They bore a gold-embossed Marine emblem at the top. The first two letters are quoted, in part, as follows:

Parris Island, South Carolina
October 6, 1942

Dear Folks:

After all these days trying to take time out to write a letter, I have finally found it. You see, I've been waiting for a chance to write in ink on this paper. Hereafter, you may just receive the letter on lined paper and in pencil.

We are hardly ever in the barracks except for sleep. Any other time it is just "in and out," with no time for anything but grabbing a rifle or something and falling in outside again.

These past four or five days have been rather hectic. We marched all over the island from quartermaster to the dentist, to the barber, to the gunnery shack, etc. Today is the first real official day of training. Those before were orientation days.

The food is good and there's plenty. The sleep is short, sweet, and welcome. The only time we lie down is to go to bed, which is at or around 10 p.m. We rise between 4 and 4:30 a.m. The haircuts are rarely over an inch in length. Most of us have blisters on our feet.

I can't say training is easy, because it isn't. Of course, my training at St. John's is helping me immeasurably.

The first couple of days down here I would find myself wondering who I was, where I came from, and what I was doing here.

I imagine that by now you have received that suitcase full of clothing and stuff. If you found any Marine Corps insignias, please don't give them away or anything, they were put in there by mistake. Please send them back in a hurry.

*   *   *

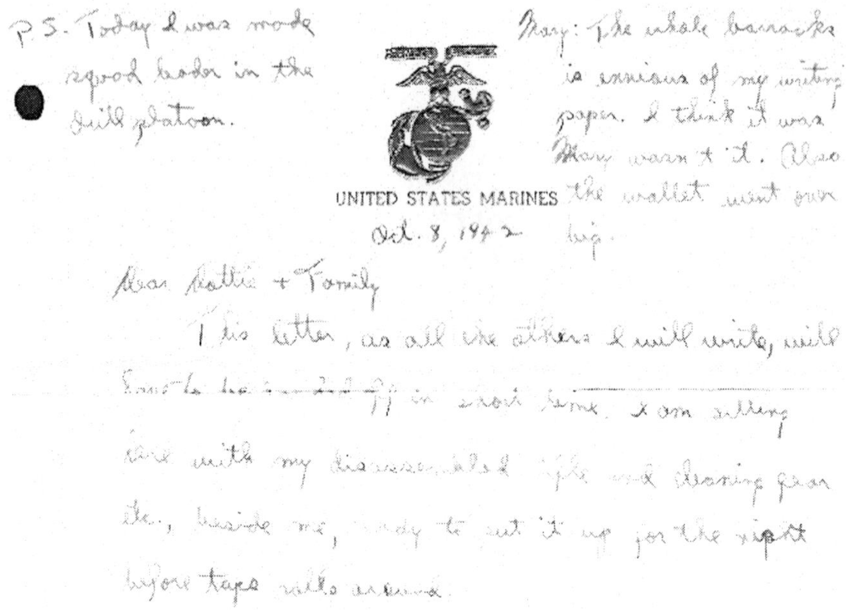

P.S. Today I was made squad leader in the drill platoon.

Mary: The whole barracks is envious of my writing paper. I think it was Mary wasn't it. Also the wallet went over big.

UNITED STATES MARINES

Oct. 8, 1942

Dear Dottie + Family

This letter, as all the others I will write, will have to be dashed off in short time. I am sitting here with my disassembled rifle and cleaning gear etc., beside me, ready to put it up for the night before taps rolls around.

October 8, 1942

Dear Dottie and Family:

This letter, as all the others I will write, will have to be dashed off in short time. I am sitting here with my disassembled rifle and cleaning gear beside me, ready to put it up for the night before taps rolls around.

As to the salutation of this letter, I haven't the time to write to each one of you in three individual letters. This one is an answer to the letter I received from Dottie yesterday.

Mary, the whole barracks is envious of this writing paper you gave me.

P.S. Today I was made a squad leader in my drill platoon.

While I was in boot camp, the oldest Marine recruit I ever heard of came to Parris Island. He was Paul Douglas, a history professor from the University of Chicago. The Marines waived their age-limit rule to allow him, at the age of 50, to join the Corps as a reservist. One evening our platoon marched down to the main station to hear him give a lecture to a packed auditorium on the historical background leading up to the Second World War.

He went through boot camp just as we all did. Later, out in the Pacific, he was wounded in one of the battles there. After the war, he ran for public office and became a United States Senator from the State of Illinois.

During the next six weeks of boot camp, at both Parris Island and New River, I sent nine more letters home. In my first letters home from boot camp, I included, at the time, some words or phrases of explanation in parentheses. Selected paragraphs from three of the boot camp letters are, as follows:

Parris Island
South Carolina
October 11, 1942

I just got back from Mass, which is about a mile-and-a-half march each way. Mass is said by a Navy chaplain in the big lyceum at the main station. (The Marine Corps has no chaplains or doctors of its own; although in many cases the chaplains and doctors are permanently stationed at Marine bases.) After Mass everyone stands, including the priest, and sings the Marine's Hymn.

A few of us have to drill today to practice as a snappy drill team. Half of our platoon has been selected as part of a Marine contingent to represent Parris Island in the Navy Day Parade at Charleston, S.C., on October 27.

*　　*　　*

October 17, 1942

Lately they've been keeping us on the run down here. Thursday, the 11th Recruit Battalion had its 10th-day inspection.

I told you, didn't I, that I am a squad leader. It is supposed to put quite a feather in one's cap to go through boot camp as a squad leader. They call us "boots" down here.

In the Marines, we call Army soldiers, "Dog faces" and Navy sailors, "Swab jockeys."

---

*　　*　　*

October 22, 1942

Everybody from our platoon and those from the other platoons who are going to march in Charleston are the envy of the other "boots." I imagine it will be quite a thrill, despite all the parading I did in high school on Constitution Avenue.

As long as we're in boot camp we have to wash our own clothes. I wash my whites every day and in that way I keep everything rotating in order.

Next week we will go into intensive training in extended-order drill. Extended order is merely squad and platoon deployment for combat. Close order is what you see in parades, etc.

While writing the original draft of this book in 1994, I found the need to further explain or clarify the text of some of the letters I had sent home after boot camp. In the chapters following, I will show current explanations of those letters in parentheses, either within the text of the letter or immediately thereafter.

While at Parris Island, each member of our platoon was photographed in Marine Corps "dress blue" jacket and white barracks cap. The photographs were sent home to our parents. Mine is shown below.

Photograph of Frank Gardner in Dress Blues
taken during boot camp at Parris Island.

CHAPTER 3

*   *   *

Camp Lejeune to Cherry Point, North Carolina

After a month at boot camp, we were ready to fire the rifle, but the firing ranges at Parris Island were completely occupied by other platoons that were also finishing their training. For this reason, ours and several other boot platoons were formed into a training battalion that was shipped off to the New River area of Camp Lejeune, North Carolina, for three weeks of rifle training and firing.

Parris Island
South Carolina
October 30, 1942

Dear Mother:
Well here it is at last! The 11th Recruit Battalion is leaving Parris Island tomorrow. We're shoving off for New River, North Carolina, for three weeks of training at the rifle range.

Everything went off all right in Charleston. We paraded on the Citadel parade grounds before 10,000 people. We slept at the Charleston Navy Yard. Those barracks were just like hotels; steam heat; thick mattresses; waxed floors (decks); plaster walls (bulkheads). That Navy chow was pretty good too.

Dottie might be interested to know that Sterling Hayden (the movie actor) *arrived here Thursday as a Marine recruit.*

Yesterday we turned in our 1903 Springfield rifles and received brand new M-1 rifles, made by Garand. We will keep these for the duration. The M-1 is a gas operated, semiautomatic, clip-fed, shoulder weapon.

*   *   *

New River
North Carolina
November 4, 1942

Dear Folks:

Our purpose here at New River is to learn to fire the rifle. Except that we sleep in large tents instead of wooden barracks, life is about the same.

This first week is called "snapping in" week. We merely practice trigger squeeze, alignment of sights, and position. Next week is also for snapping in, but in addition we fire small 22 caliber rifles for practice. After these two weeks of snapping in, we go 15 miles to the main range for actual firing and qualifications with our 30 caliber rifles.

*　　*　　*

New River, November 11, 1942

Dear Family:

I got Dottie's letter yesterday and today I received mother's letter and the insignias. Thanks a lot for them. Speaking of losing things, I thought I had lost that pipe you gave me, Dottie. For the last three days I have been looking all over for it. Just tonight I found it, tucked away in my seabag. A Marine seabag is made of brown canvass and is about one foot square inside. It stands three feet high, when filled. (The Navy seabag is white.) *Into it goes all we own. My pipe had slipped very far into it. Here in New River we live out of our seabags. All we have inside the tent are seven beds, kerosene stove, seven rifles, and seven seabags.*

---

*　　*　　*

New River, November 15, 1942

Dear Folks:

Platoon 816 is now residing comfortably, for a week, anyway, in the brick, steam-heated barracks at the 30-caliber rifle range, which is 15 miles south of Tent City, the school range. It is about 8:00 p.m. on Sunday night and we are all squared away in our new quarters.

(Same letter)

> *New River, November 16, 1942*
>
> *Our platoon is scheduled to fire the rifle for the first time this afternoon. This morning we have work to do. I am scheduled to go with a group to the armory. Others will perform duties such as mess, policing, or salvage.*

We spent the week of November 16 firing the rifle at distances of 200 to 500 yards. In addition, we all took our turns working in the butts, which were deep trenches where the targets were housed. The duty there involved marking targets to show the men on the firing line where their bullets had hit. In case of a miss, we waved a red flag called "Maggie's drawers." We then patched the holes in the targets and raised them back up on the parapet for the next round of firing.

After a week of practice, we fired for qualification on the last day. I scored 294, missing expert by six points. This meant I had qualified in the middle class, above marksman, called sharpshooter. My firing coach was more disappointed than I that I hadn't made expert. I took solace in pinning onto my uniform the sharpshooter's badge that my father had in World War One.

On two occasions over the next two years I did fire expert, scoring 310 out of a possible 340 on September 2, 1944, at a rifle range in Hawaii. However, during the war I never did get around to replacing my father's old sharpshooter medal with the one for expert. Some forty years later, I had my son, Tommy, himself then a Marine rifle expert, pick up an expert medal for me at the Post Exchange on the Quantico Marine Base. Both medals are on display now, along with some others, in a shadow box at home.

I am shown (above left), in Marine Corps uniform, wearing the same, actual sharpshooter medal my father wore twenty-four years earlier in World War One.

My father (above right), Ivory V. Gardner, in U. S. Army uniform, is shown in 1919 with Marie Bruen, my mother, before they were married. Above his sharpshooter medal, is shown the campaign ribbon with one battle star that he earned in France in 1918. I never really got to know my father, since I was only two years old when he died from a work-related accident in 1924.

One day in boot camp, all the men in our platoon were given a test on radio signals. As we listened to the Morse Code dots and dashes, we were to identify those sounds that were identical and those that were not. Those few of us who scored highest in that test were marked for radio training. Further testing was done to identify men with other skills and aptitudes. They would be sent for training in various other specialized fields related to aviation.

On Saturday, November 21, the day after we fired the rifle for qualification, we were no longer "boots," but full-fledged Marines.

There was no formal graduation ceremony, such as Parris Island puts on traditionally in peacetime.

At noon, 130 of us earmarked for aviation left the 11th Recruit Battalion and went to the Marine Corps Air Station, Cherry Point, North Carolina. Of that number, I was among thirteen men scheduled for aviation radio training. The 840 Marines remaining in the battalion were to return to Tent City, awaiting assignments to guard duty, mess duty, or infantry training.

After about two weeks of standing by, we thirteen radio trainees began taking some instruction at Cherry Point. Meanwhile, I learned that my older sister, Dorothy, had entered the novitiate of the Daughters of Charity of Saint Vincent de Paul on December 8, 1942, in Baltimore, Maryland. Of seven letters sent home from Cherry Point during two months, three were sent to Dorothy at Mount Hope Retreat in Baltimore. Two of those are, as follows:

Cherry Point, North Carolina,
January 3, 1943

Dear Dottie:

You know, in the service we are allowed to hear Mass and receive communion in the afternoon. New Year's Day marked the second time I had such an experience, the Feast of the Immaculate Conception being the first. Those afternoon masses are said at 5:30.

A group of us got together and formed a small choir. We sang the Mass of the Angels for Midnight Mass at Christmas. My prayers were for you, mother, and Mary.

---

*   *   *

Cherry Point, January 13, 1943

Dear Dottie:

Our day here goes like this. Rise at 6:00; exercise from 6:15 to 6:30; morning chow between 6:30 and 7:50; Morse Code from 7:50 to 9:30; close-order drill from 9:30 to 9:50; Naval Radio Procedure from 9:50 to 11:15; clean up radio school until 11:30; one hour for mid-day chow; Morse Code from 12:30 to 1:45; Naval Radio Procedure from 1:45 to 3:00; one half hour to clean up the radio school; Judo from 3:30 to 4:30. Then we're off for the remainder of the day, with time for evening chow, mail call, letter writing, movies, and Taps, in that order.

CHAPTER 4

*   *   *

Radio School at Texas A & M College

By January 18, our class of radio trainees numbered forty-seven. We were shipped off to the Marine Air Detachment, Naval Training School, Texas A & M College, College Station, Texas. Selected paragraphs from some of my letters home follow:

Texas A & M
January 26, 1943

This campus is immense, all laid out in streets, wooded lanes, walks, lawns, shrubbery, etc.
We are housed in a group of new buildings of concrete and brick construction. We live three to a room.

---

*   *   *

> Texas A & M
> *February 5, 1943*
>
> *The Marines here are taking the radio operator's course for aviation. Half of the sailors are taking the same course for use with the fleet. The other sailors are taking radio material and radar.*
>
> *There are about 8,000 Aggies here; 1500 sailors; and 400 Marines.*
>
> *Compared to the sailors, what we lack in numbers is made up in our general appearance and military bearing, in and out of ranks. I've noticed how the Aggies will stop and watch when a unit of Marines is performing close-order drill. The sailors are a congenial bunch of guys with their personality and good fellowship, but they show a lack of organization. We in the Marine detachment maintain a system much like a regular Marine Corps base, as the sergeant told us we would have to do.*
>
> *We have a half-hour of calisthenics every morning, except Sunday, before chow. After a full day at school, we have a half-hour of close-order drill every afternoon before chow. All of this is regardless of whether or not the sailors do, which they don't very often.*
>
> *The spirit of the Aggies is like what you hear about at Notre Dame, especially during football season. It's a tradition here that during football games the Aggies in the stands will remain standing for the entire game, sitting down only when there is a "time out" and at half time.*

(They call this, "The 12th man," a tradition that started at Texas A & M FVG)

We Marines going through the Naval Training School took the same course in radio operating as did the sailors going out to the fleet. Most of us would be assigned as flying radio operators aboard dive bombers or torpedo bombers in Marine Air Squadrons. Nevertheless, we still had to learn to use the typewriter and to receive Morse code on the typewriter, since there was the chance that any one of us might be assigned to use such equipment at a Marine Corps Air Station.

Texas A & M
February 21, 1943

I've been busy the past week. I had been going over to school at nights trying to pick up more accuracy in my typing and speed in code receiving. My average typing speed is around 35 words per minute (wpm), although on some assignments (the easy ones) I have gone as high as 42 wpm.

I suppose I'll have to file income tax this year for the first time. To make sure, I've sent letters to: the N.Y.A., the District of Columbia Government, Welfare and Recreation Association, Shepherd Park Pharmacy, and National Drug Company, inquiring as to my earnings so I can arrive at a total. I know how much I made from the British because I received only one check for $10.95.

By this time, my letters to the family involved much duplication. I was reciting the same information to mother in Washington, Dorothy in Baltimore, and Mary at St. Joseph's College in Emmitsburg, Maryland.

Texas A & M
March 9, 1943

Dear Mother:

After writing Dottie and Mary last night (I owed each of them a letter), I had planned on writing you, but time did not permit. It was just as well, though, for today I received your long letter and I'll have plenty to talk about.

So, Dorothy is now in Emmitsburg. Well, that means the letter I sent last night ought to be forwarded. That's a good picture of her.

Yes, I've been thinking all along about going back to college when this is all over. I've been thinking about how long it'll be before it is over. After an experience like this, college might not be an easy thing to go back to. When people get into a set pattern of living, they don't relish the idea of reverting to that which they left many years before. Depending on many things, I am liable to choose this Marine Corps as my profession. The war will tell!

*   *   *

Texas A & M
March 19, 1943

Dear Mother:

The Army has taken over A & M College as of today. The contract juniors and seniors are being sent off to camp. They will receive government-issue (G.I.) clothing and some inoculation shots, and then come back here to resume their regular college courses. So, they were promised, and so the Aggies hope.

> *My typing speed is really increasing and I seem to have a good rhythm. I still have to cut down on my errors but I'm doing 40 words a minute regularly now; and that's the requirement for a rating, as far as typing goes.*
>
> *This week I've been going over to school at night to improve my code sending. I'm taking 16 wpm in code with a stick (pencil). Will start code typing next week.*
>
> *Well, I learned that my earnings for 1942 were not enough to warrant my paying an income tax.*

*   *   *

> *Texas A & M*
> *April 6, 1943*
>
> **Dear Mother:**
>
> *This will be a short letter. I do not have much time for writing these days. I have started teaching a small class of sailors how to swim. I hold classes on Mondays, Wednesdays, and Fridays from 7 to 8 at night.*
>
> *I am still working hard in school. Enclosed, please find another $20 to invest in your savings plan.*

*   *   *

April 25, 1943

Dear Mother and Mary:

I haven't had much time to do anything the past week. I've been going to night school every night for code typing. Our theory and procedure homework assignments have been getting heavy. That's why I'm writing you both in one letter.

Concerning this night school that's taking so much of my time, code typing really had me on the go. I had been doing all right with a "stick," at 20 wpm; but then the synchronization of the code and the typing puzzled me. Sgt. Hendricks, our instructor, put me on the right track last week, though. He showed me where I was going about it wrong. Right now I'm taking 14 wpm. Whether I can get up to the required 22 words per minute for a corporal rating is a matter for time to tell. I'll certainly try hard though.

It was a shock to hear of Aunt Leo's death. I wired flowers and a telegram. I imagine Uncle Lud received them. The only address I could think of was Popkins Lane, Groveton, Virginia.

Mary, they were sailors I was teaching to swim, not Aggies. My typing speed is 45 wpm now. Please don't forget my birth certificate.

I haven't heard from Dorothy since she left Mt. Hope. Shall I just write to her at the Mother House in Emmitsburg and address it Sister Dorothy?

*   *   *

Texas A & M
June 9, 1943

Dear Mother:

You know, in the Navy, they have a system of marking where 4.0 is equivalent to 100%. My averages in Theory and Procedure are fairly high: 3.84 Theory; 3.7 Procedure. Typing is low, at 3.2. I think my marks are good enough to warrant my getting a rating if I can copy 22 wpm or above. I am now at 20 wpm.

Today I reached a height that I've been striving for a long time and working hard at, too. I got a 4.0 in code sending. There were nine 4.0s in the class of 102.

*   *   *

Texas A & M
June 19, 1943

Dear Mother:

Today I graduated. I received a diploma from Texas A & M College, stating that I have satisfactorily completed the course and am now a qualified radio operator. Also, I received a Marine Corps warrant stating that I have been promoted (from private) to the rating of corporal. Out of a total of 158 men graduating, I was 18th in the class. There were 39 corporals rated. I think that's the hardest rate I'll ever earn.

Under separate cover I mailed you the diploma and the warrant. I enclosed them in a "Leatherneck" magazine. Also enclosed, was a "diploma" of good will given to us at our graduation dance by the people of the nearby town of Bryan. (Apparently, the diplomas and the warrant became lost in the mail or misplaced, for I never saw them again. FVG, 1994)

The graduation dance for Naval and Marine personnel has long been a standby here at A & M It is sponsored and chaperoned mostly by Knights of Columbus officials. The girls are brought in from nearby Houston, Dallas, Fort Worth, and, of course, Bryan.

Today, we're just sitting around, waiting for our orders to come from Washington. So, I still don't know where I'm going.

I'm really happy. I guess you are too.

Author shown in both photos at Texas
A & M College, Spring of 1943

CHAPTER 5

* * *

Quantico, Virginia, to Cherry Point

> *Texas A and M*
> *June 20, 1943*
>
> *Dear Mother:*
> *Just a quick note to tell you that I'm being sent to Quantico, Virginia, for duty at the Marine Corps Air Station there.*

At the Quantico Air Station my first assignment was assisting some electronic technicians to install radar on a few *Mitchell* medium bombers the Marine Corps was beginning to use. The North American Company manufactured these airplanes. They were designated B-25 by the Army and PBJ by the Navy and Marines.

Radar was a secret weapon developed by the British and American forces in World War II. The word, "radar" is an acronym, taken from the phrase: *r*adio *d*etecting *a*nd *r*anging. The system involved an electronic device that emitted ultrahigh-frequency radio signals into the air. They, in turn, would strike an object out in space, such as another airplane. The signal would reflect back to a receiver at the source, thereby detecting the object and recording its direction and distance.

Later on, I joined a small group of radio operators taking classes in aircraft and surface-vessel recognition. Excerpts from some of my letters are as follows:

Quantico, Virginia
July 21, 1943

I imagine I can tell you that I am in here, but I can't give anyone any details or such like of what we're doing with it: aircraft radar. It's all confidential work and the hangar is always closely guarded. No one is allowed inside the hangar except we who have work to do there.

Now that I am no longer in school, I can make inquiries about getting into Officer Candidate School (OCS). The other day I was in the top sergeant's office to see about getting permission to talk to Captain Spears about OCS. Everything seemed OK until he looked at my Army classification test from boot camp. My grade was 109. He said, that according to a new letter of instruction, the grade necessary for recommendation was 110. I asked him what could be done. He said, "Nothing." So, that was that!

We just got paid last night, so enclosed please find $10.

* * *

> *Quantico, Virginia*
> *August 2, 1943*
>
> *Excuse the pencil. I can't find my pen.*
> *Well, we're progressing rapidly now in our recognition training. So far we've been on nothing but U. S. ships and airplanes. Yesterday we had a test on battleships. I missed one out of 24, the second highest in our group. We've taken up ten classes of battleships, five classes of heavy cruisers, and 17 airplanes.*
> *You know, I think I'd like to get some flight action before I get into OCS. I don't think we're going to be here too long.*

Later in August, mother, who had spent fifteen years working as a civilian for the Navy Department, was accepted as an officer candidate in the U. S. Navy Reserve. She was sent to Smith College in New York for a three-month training course. Graduates of the Military and Naval Academies, who had gone through four-year college programs for their commissions, used to refer to wartime officers from the three-month courses as, "Ninety-day wonders." Civilians also used the term derisively or jokingly.

By November, mother had finished training and returned to Washington as an ensign in the Navy. She went back to work in the Navy Department's Bureau of Ordnance where she had worked previously as a civilian. This time she had a more responsible position.

Quantico
November 14, 1943

Dear Mother:

If you are able to get hold of any pictures of planes (not necessarily Navy) and ships, (battleships, cruisers, aircraft carriers, and destroyers) I could use them in my notebook. **

We have had four tests so far, and my average is 97.5. If I can only keep it up on German and Japanese planes, I'll be doing O.K. Although this is more of an instruction course than a formal school, I imagine it's still a good idea to strive for perfection.

I'm getting only $10 next payday, so I'll have to ask you for as much of the $65.00 as you can rustle up for me by next weekend. This bond-a-month program is really knocking my pay for a loop. Also, the quartermaster must have taken a lump sum in payment for some clothing I had to buy from him to make up my original Government Issue.

You see, I want to get some presents and things to give for Christmas. Also I want to do some shopping on my own before I ship out. I'll be seeing you this Saturday.

** *(Mother found a booklet for me to use at the time: "The (1942) Ships and Aircraft of the U. S. Fleet". Now, about sixty-five years later, I am using it again to show ships and planes in this book.)*

> *Quantico, Virginia*
> *November 23, 1943*
>
> *Dear Mother:*
> *This will be our hardest week in recognition. These Japanese names are something terrible; and many of their planes resemble each other very closely.*
> *I didn't intend to make this very lengthy because I have to do some more studying.*
> *We'll be shipping out at the end of next week, so I'll be up to visit you on Saturday for two days.*

When I visited mother in Washington on the weekend, a sidewalk photographer on F Street snapped our picture. (Shown here.) We proceeded on to Brooks Studio, where we had a photograph taken in our military uniforms.

The print is framed and mounted on the wall of my den at home. It is shown on the next page.

After leaving the studio that day, we saw a newspaper being sold on the street. The shocking banner headline across the top of the front page read: "**1,000 MARINES**." The article reported that 1,000 Marines had just been killed in one three-day island victory. It was on a small atoll, called Tarawa in the Pacific.

In December 1943, I returned to Cherry Point as a qualified radio operator. I assumed I would be assigned to a squadron of Marine aircraft, flying as a radio gunner. This assignment could have been from an air base in the South Pacific or from an aircraft carrier. A likely aircraft would have been a dive-bomber made by the Douglas Company, designated SBD, the *Dauntless*. Another might have been the newer SB2C *Helldiver,* made by the Curtiss Company. Also, radio gunners were needed in torpedo bombers, first made by Grumman, designated TBF, and later by General Motors, as TBM. Both were called the *Avenger*.

DOUGLAS SBD-3 Scout Bomber from VS-2 (The LEXINGTON)

CURTISS XSB2C-1 Scout Bomber

Sunday —
Dec. 5, 1943

Dear Mother;

This address is more or less
temporary, I think. I think our whole
bunch here
our kind of an warning group.
Quarters is due to get into

U. S. Marine Corps Air Station
Cherry Point, North Carolina
December 5, 1943

Dear Mother:

This address is more or less temporary. I think our whole bunch from Quantico is due to get into some kind of an air warning group. (See December 15 letter in next chapter.)

Well, I got here just in time for singing at Midnight Mass. Even this morning (Sunday) they had me in the choir. As I walked into the chapel the chaplain's assistant spotted me right away. He remembered me from last year, and asked me to help with the singing. There are many Lady Marines here now, and the choir has more female voices than male.

CHAPTER 6

*   *   *

Air Warning Squadron Five

At Cherry Point, in December 1943, we learned that we would not be flying in dive-bombers or torpedo bombers. Instead, we would be assigned as radio operators on the ground, carrying cumbersome radios on our backs, called "Walkie Talkies." We would make amphibious landings with Marines on enemy-held islands and provide air warning to our troops ashore.

Corporal F. V. Gardner
AWS-5 (AT), 1st MAWG
3rd MAW, FMF, USMCAS
Cherry Point, N. Carolina
December 15, 1943

Ensign Marie B. Gardner, USNR
1020 19th Street, Northwest
Washington, D. C.

Dear Mother

My new address translates into the following: Air Warning Squadron Five (Air Transportable) of the First Marine Air Warning Group, (1st MAWG) which is in the Third Marine Air Wing, (3RD MAW) attached to the Fleet Marine Force (FMF). Some address! It is really a great outfit.

That $10 certainly will help me. Thanks. Due to all this transferring, I'm not going to get paid until the 5th of January.

The other day I was thinking about the desire of some young men to become officers. For my part, I want to prove myself as an enlisted man, a good enlisted man, and then I'll be able to make a better officer.

This new outfit that I'm in, AWS-5 (A T), is a small, fast moving, highly specialized unit. Now that it has its full quota of men, it holds each of us indispensable. I don't think they'd let anyone leave the outfit, even for OCS. So, I'm not going to bother about pestering them any further in that regard.

By the way, the commanding officer of the 1st MAWG is Colonel Baylon, the "last man off Wake Island" before it was captured by the Japanese. He is the author of the book bearing that title.

In the choir, Bab, the lady director, has me singing bass. The tenors are so good and plentiful and the basses are so scarce that I do better filling in there for the carols. Of course for the Mass of the Angels, everyone sings the melody in unison; and I know the Latin by heart from St. Joseph's Home and School. We're having a big blizzard down here.

*   *   *

Cherry Point, N. C.
December 26, 1943

Dear Mother and Mary:

Before Midnight Mass we sang carols, and during the service we sang the regular Gregorian Chant's Mass of the Angels. Everything came off well. Our "Gesu Bambino" was very good. We also sang for the ten o'clock mass on Christmas morning.

Mary, as for my voice, it's nothing exceptional, just good enough to serve the purpose. I learned my bass parts well, but most of my value to the choir was in my proficiency concerning the (Latin) *Mass of the Angels.*

Most of today I've spent washing and mending my clothes. The laundry service here is terrible, so I don't bother to rely on it.

We are receiving specialized combat conditioning courses. Sometime soon we'll be shoving off to Georgia or New River for a week's training in landing operations. Later, we'll be shoving off for the West Coast.

About half of the men in our new outfit, Air Warning Squadron Five (AT), were radar specialists, who would carry portable components of electronic equipment on their backs. One of our five-man radar teams could come ashore and piece together the various components they were carrying, such as receiver unit, viewing scope, antennae, and hand-powered generator. Within minutes they would have a small radar station in operation inside their camouflaged tent.

The "air transportable" tag on our unit designation, indicated that we could be flown by air transport, together with all of our radio and electronic equipment, from one place of operations to another.

Our radar operators were trained to detect enemy aircraft at a distance on their radar screens. Then, as the airplanes came closer, we radio operators, trained in aircraft recognition, could study them with our binoculars, identify them, and report their actions to our commanders. Being highly mobile, we might even set up observation posts on small, uninhabited South Pacific islands in support of landings nearby, or so we thought. As things turned out, we never entered the South Pacific Area, which was south of the Equator. We stayed in the Central Pacific, north of the Equator, the whole time we were overseas.

The first four air warning squadrons, designated AWS-1 through AWS-4, were already setting up on Pacific-island bases secured earlier in 1943. They, with their motorized heavy equipment, would remain in place indefinitely at those locations. Our outfit, AWS-5 (AT), was destined to go ashore with invasion troops on some island yet to be taken from the enemy.

Perhaps another ten more air warning squadrons were planned. Most would be for permanent installations, with their heavy electronic equipment in large motorized vehicles. Every fifth squadron formed, those with number designations divisible by five, would be like ours, highly mobile and air transportable, designed to go ashore with invasion troops.

In letters home I didn't go into such details because some of it was military information the family didn't need to know, and the rest of it I didn't know myself at the time.

Cherry Point, N. C.
January 9, 1944

Dear Mother:

Well, tomorrow we're scheduled to fly down to Georgia. We are going to make a practice "assault" landing on a small island off the coast, coming in from the ocean by landing craft. We'll then set up our equipment and go to work with our air warning operations. We'll each carry a full pack, containing a shelter half, blanket roll, and K rations. The other gear we carry includes helmet, cartridge belt, gas mask, bayonet, shovel, and rifle. The estimated weight of everything, that I must carry, including a field radio, is over 80 pounds.

So, even though we are aviation specialists, we'll be going into action with the amphibious assault forces. This is really a rugged outfit. I wish I could tell you more about it.

In January 1944, I was promoted to sergeant and put in charge of a squad of seven men.

Cherry Point
January 25, 1944

Dear Mother:

We've been fairly busy here lately, with forced marches, obstacle courses, and rifle inspections.

Everything went OK on the rifle range. We fired just enough rounds from two, three and five hundred yards to "zero-in" our rifles: 28 rounds all together. I scored 131 out of 140, based on five points maximum for each round.

I have drawn up a code to let you know "where I am" when I write from the Pacific in letters that must be censored:

Hawaii:	*Hal*	*Marshalls:*	*Mark*
Solomons:	*Joe*	*Gilberts:*	*Bill*
Formosa:	*Jim*	*Australia:*	*Bob*
New Zealand:	*Fred*	*Truk:*	*Tom*
Phillippines:	*Phil*		

I'll use the third paragraph of my letter to mention one of these names to let you know "where I am."

For the next few days we're going to be very busy, loading all of our heavy gear and supplies. We'll probably be working night and day, so if I get any chance to write, it'll be in hastily written notes.

I'm going to close now and prepare for tomorrow's formal inspection.

As things turned out, my "whereabouts code" came into play for only one of the nine locations listed in my letter. That location was Hawaii.

CHAPTER 7

*   *   *

Cherry Point to Camp Miramar, California

At the end of January 1944, AWS-5 was set to move to the West Coast. We would no longer be part of the Third Marine Air Wing based at Cherry Point.

Cherry Point, North Carolina
January 31, 1944

Dear Mother:

All our heavy equipment is loaded on the trains and has started on its way to the West Coast. (We would carry our walkie-talkies and all of our personal battle gear on board the transport planes. FVG 1998)

We got paid this morning, and tonight there are four good-sized poker games going on in the barracks. I've played a little, but I avoid the "professional" contests. There are better things I can do with my money.

Because we were "air transportable," we didn't take the train to the West Coast, as did most Marine units. Our squadron of 168 officers and men boarded several R4D transport planes at Cherry Point, North Carolina, on February 8, 1944. We flew with full battle gear to the El Toro Marine Corps Air Station in California, where we landed on February 12. According to the four postcards I mailed home along the way, we had a refueling stop at the Municipal Airport in Atlanta, Georgia; a two-day layover at Fort Worth Army Air Field in Texas due to bad weather; and another refueling stop at an Army field in Arizona.

Shown here is the Douglas R4D *Skytrain*. It was designated *C-47* by

the Army. Hundreds of these *DC-3* airplanes were used by the nation's commercial airlines beginning around 1940.

U. S. MARINE CORPS
★ AVIATION ★

Feb. 20, 1944

Dear Mother,
    All last week we were on maneuvers
up and down these hills around this

Camp Miramar
San Diego, California
February 20, 1944

Dear Mother:

All last week we were on maneuvers up and down these hills around this San Diego area. We finished up the week by firing on the rifle range at Camp Matthews. I did rather well, better than at Cherry Point.

This week we have more field training and some practice in amphibious landings.

*   *   *

Camp Miramar, California
March 2, 1944

Dear Mother:

We have gone through two courses at Camp Elliot with machine guns being fired over our heads as we crawl through barbed wire, mud holes, and ditches. Land mines and grenades are set off nearby to give additional realistic effect as we slither forward on our bellies. At the end, we all look like mud pies. It takes us all of our evenings to clean our rifles.

Otherwise, we have been trooping up and down all these hills, as usual. We have made two practice landings with the regular assault troops. Occasionally, we go out into the field on an all-night problem.

>  *Enclosed you will find my Third Marine Air Wing shoulder patch. We were ordered to remove them from our uniforms.*
>
> *We are going to leave here very soon for overseas. Today, I have to take a working party down to the harbor to start loading our ship.*

When out in the field, each of us carried a "shelter half" in his backpack. Two shelter halves, when placed together, made up one pup tent for two Marines. By this time, our white underclothing, which we called "skivvies," had all been dyed a dull green color for camouflage.

(Typed letter)

Camp Miramar, March 25, 1944

Dear Mother:

The reason for the typewriter is that I am Sergeant of the Guard for the day, and it is easier to stay awake tonight while I'm typing. My duties in this capacity require me to stay up all night long. Now that Taps has sounded and the tent area is secured for the night, I've decided to do some letter writing, something I never seem to be caught up on. Also, as you most probably know, one can think faster at the typewriter.

We made another practice landing last week. We're getting better all the time. The last few days we have been doing some field training such as we did at St. Simon's Island in Georgia back in January. We set up a few five-man radio outposts in the 100-mile stretch between here and Los Angeles. I was in charge of one about 25 miles south of Long Beach on top of a large hill overlooking the ocean. We stayed three days and nights, reporting airplane sightings, eating K rations, and sleeping in our pup tents.

In San Diego, a few Sundays ago, I was on my way back to the base in the late afternoon. A sailor on the street stopped me and asked if I would like to go to a private home for a few hours, enjoy myself, have some refreshments, and be driven back downtown. Upon my consent, he ushered me to a large seven-passenger Packard. A civilian driver and six sailors were already inside. The driver told us the "home" belonged to a rich, elderly woman from Los Angeles, whose contribution to the war effort was to befriend servicemen and to give them a "home" to visit.

Of course, we seven expected we'd be the only ones at the place, and I figured that seven was too many anyway. When we got there, we found at least seven *times* seven ahead of us. They were all gathered in a very large living room, seated on chairs facing in the same direction. You probably know what I'm coming to already, don't you? Yes, they even had a little evangelical meeting. After refreshments, those who wanted to go to vesper services were driven over in cars. I, as did the majority of the fellows, graciously withdrew.

I imagine that "Mother Layne," as she was called, does a certain amount of good in a small way, but her efforts can influence only a small percentage of the men she contacts. You will probably get some correspondence from her, as she took all of our names and the names and addresses of our folks. *(Apparently nothing ever came of this, for mother never mentioned it. FVG 1998)*

*   *   *

Camp Miramar, California
March 27, 1944

Dear Mother:

    Today I received the chessboard. Thanks a lot. I know how to play a little; picked it up at Texas A & M. I hope I'm an accomplished player when I get home. Perhaps we can have a contest.

    This will be the last letter I write you while in the States. I'm going to start another letter, and add a little each day; then send it to you when we reach our destination.

    I think the walking picture is very good of both of us. The fellows think I look a lot like you.

    "The Sullivans" is playing at the movies tonight. I've heard it's good, so I think I'll go see it.

    I'll be seeing you in the newsreels.

Before boarding ship, all 168 members of Air Warning Squadron Five assembled for a group photograph. I am shown to the right of the break, the fourth person down from the top.

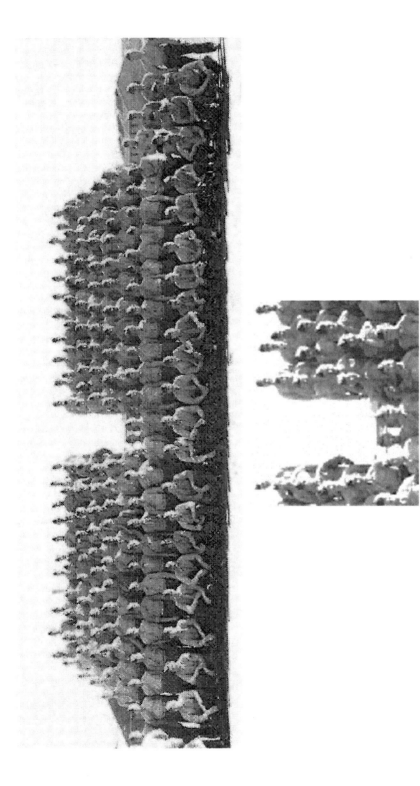

PART II

Remembering Saipan, Iwo Jima, and Okinawa

General Pacific Battle Information

Central Pacific Area Commands:

Principal Marine Corps and Army Units (Except for Tenth Army on Okinawa)

Fifth Amphibious Corps (VAC):
Lt. General Holland M. Smith, USMC

Gilbert Islands 1943	Principal atolls:	Tarawa	Second Marine Division
		Makin	27th Infantry Division
Marshall Islands 1944	Principal atolls:	Kwajalein	4th Marine Division
			7th Infantry Division
		Eniwetok	22nd Marine Regiment
			105th Infantry Regiment
Mariana Islands 1944	Principal islands	Saipan	Second Marine Division
			Fourth Marine Division
		Tinian	Fourth Marine Division
			Second Marine Division

Fifth Amphibious Corps (VAC):
Major General Harry Schmidt, USMC

Bonin (Volcano) Islands 1945	Iwo Jima	Fourth Marine Division
		Fifth Marine Division
		Third Marine Division

Third Amphibious Corps (IIIAC):
Major General Roy S Geiger, USMC

Mariana Islands 1944		Guam	Third Marine Division
			First Marine Provisional
Brigade			77th Infantry Division
Palau Islands 1944	Principal islands	Peleliu	First Marine Division
		Angaur	81st Infantry Division
Ryukyu Islands		Okinawa	First Marine Division
(Marine Divisions)			Sixth Marine Division
1945			Second Marine Division

First Marine Division
Guadalcanal, New Britain, Peleliu,
Okinawa

Second Marine Division
Guadalcanal, Tarawa, Saipan,
Tinian, Okinawa

Third Marine Division
Bougainville, Guam, Iwo Jima

Fourth Marine Division
Roi-Namur, Saipan, Tinian,
Iwo Jima

Fifth Marine Division
Iwo Jima

Sixth Marine Division
Okinawa

U. S. S. Wasp, CV 18, commissioned in 1943 (Essex Class) (The ninth Navy ship named Wasp)

27,100 tons, 872 feet in length, aircraft, 80 plus (I recall a top speed of 35 knots.)

Among many engagements, she provided air support for ground troops on Saipan and Iwo Jima.

U.S.S. Enterprise, CV 6, commissioned in 1938 (Her sailors called her the "Big E.")

19,900 tons, 809 feet in length, speed, 34 knots; aircraft, 81

Among many battles, she provided air support for troops on Saipan, Iwo Jima, and Okinawa.

Data on aircraft carriers is from the 1942 publication, "Ships and Aircraft of the U. S. Fleet." After 1942, data is from the Dictionary of American Naval Fighting Ships (DANFS), and as I recall. FVG

CHAPTER 8

* * *

Ready for Battle in the Central Pacific

Air Warning Squadron Five (AWS-5) boarded the new *United States Ship Wasp* at North Island, San Diego, California, on March 27, 1944. This ship was one of the Essex Class, among the largest and fastest aircraft carriers in the Navy at the time. It replaced the previous, smaller *Wasp*, which had been sunk during a battle in the Solomon Islands in September 1942.

The new *Wasp* had a crew of 3,000 officers and men, including Navy lieutenant, John Aspinwall Roosevelt, son of President Franklin D. Roosevelt. Besides our 168 officers and men, there were three other small units, adding up to about 1,000 troops being transported. Most of the men slept on the hangar deck underneath the airplanes that were stored there.

Aboard aircraft carriers, Navy planes always had their wings folded when they were stored on either the flight deck or on the hanger deck, just below. On this cruise, the *Wasp* was carrying twice its normal load of aircraft.

We cruised westward and docked on April 3rd at Pearl Harbor, Oahu, Territory of Hawaii. AWS-5 was assigned to the Marine Corps Air Station at Ewa on the same island. Ewa is pronounced somewhat like "ever," without the "r."

In letters home from overseas we used a return address, regardless of our particular location. The address included name; rank for officers, rating for enlisted men; unit designation; and Fleet Post Office (FPO). We wrote that information every time on the top of the letter as well as on the outside of the envelope. The Fleet Post Office would forward letters to us regardless of the base or ship we might be on. In this book, I will not repeat the address with each letter. For the benefit of those reading this book, I will show in parentheses the place where I wrote the letter if it is not obvious from the text.

Because we were overseas in wartime, we did not seal our letters, so that our officers could read, or censor, our outgoing mail. There were times I sent money home, trusting the censors not to take it, and they never did. They would use razor blades to cut out forbidden words, such as names of organizations or places we had been. This was to prevent the enemy from learning of troop movements in the event our mail became intercepted. In this book I will show: **BLANK**, in bold capital letters, where the censor had made a cut. I will then show the deleted word(s) underlined.

(Written at MCAS EWA)

Sgt. F. V. Gardner
Air Warning Sqdn. 5 (AT)
C/O Fleet Post Office
San Francisco, California
April 6, 1944

Dear Mother:

Well, here I am healthy and happy. I like the place as well as any other I've been to.

We had a pleasant voyage on the way over. The Navy chow was very good sometimes, and very poor at other times. There's one thing you have to hand them. They always have good coffee. I remember you telling me once before, that Navy people have a passion for good coffee, and that the Navy goes to great pains to get the best coffee on the market.

Right before we shipped out, I ran into Hal Mundsen in **BLANK:** *San Diego. He had just made 2nd Class, so we took a little time out to celebrate.*

(Regarding coffee, on board ship, we learned to ask for a cup of coffee as the sailors did, by saying, "A cup of Joe.") FVG

(Regarding Hal Mundsen, this was a coded message. See my "whereabouts code" in letter dated January 25, 1944, on Page 58.) FVG

In the case of my first letter to mother, the censor had cut out *San Diego*. However, neither he nor the enemy could have known that I was informing mother of my whereabouts in Hawaii by using the name of Hal in the third paragraph of my letter.

For other places where I landed later, I could never apply the "whereabouts code" to my letters. I had made up my list of "whereabouts islands" based on past military history and some uninformed guesswork on my part. I thought I would be landing on islands in the South Pacific, or the Marshalls, that we had already captured; then advancing island by island from there. I had not even considered striking a thousand miles across the Central Pacific to islands we had never heard of.

As things turned out, I entered Pearl Harbor four times, crossed that vast ocean four times, and sailed on nine different Navy ships: *Wasp, Sheridan, J. Franklin Bell, Thurston,* LST-784, LST-84, *Bladen, Rawlins, and Copahee.* In the process, I landed and fought on three small islands in the far Pacific with strange sounding names.

Early in the war, the Navy had identified the South Pacific as the area for its initial offensive to halt the Japanese advance toward Australia. It began with the First Marine Division's landing on Guadalcanal in the Solomon Islands on August 7, 1942.

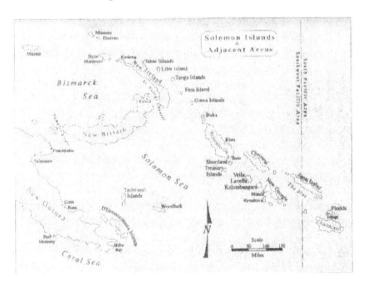

In November of the same year, General Douglas MacArthur's U. S. Army, along with some Australian troops, began a new offensive on New Guinea toward the Philippines. This was identified as the Southwest

Pacific Area, separating the Navy's South Pacific Area at the Solomon Islands. By mid-1943, our military strategy in the Pacific had changed. General MacArthur's offensive in the Southwest Pacific would continue moving toward the Philippines, "leapfrogging" his Army troops along the 1,500-mile northern coast of New Guinea.

A separate offensive would advance across the Central Pacific,

By the end of 1943, the Navy-Marine amphibious operations had captured, bypassed, or neutralized the key islands in the Solomons. The South Pacific offensive in the Solomon Islands would be discontinued in favor of a new offensive across the middle of the Pacific Ocean toward Japan.

This offensive, under the command of Fleet Admiral Chester W. Nimitz, using mostly Marine amphibious forces, would strike first at the Gilbert Islands in late 1943. On November 23, 1943, the Second Marine Division captured Betio and its one airfield of the Tarawa Atoll. This was a ferocious three-day battle, where 990 Marines were killed and 2,300, wounded.

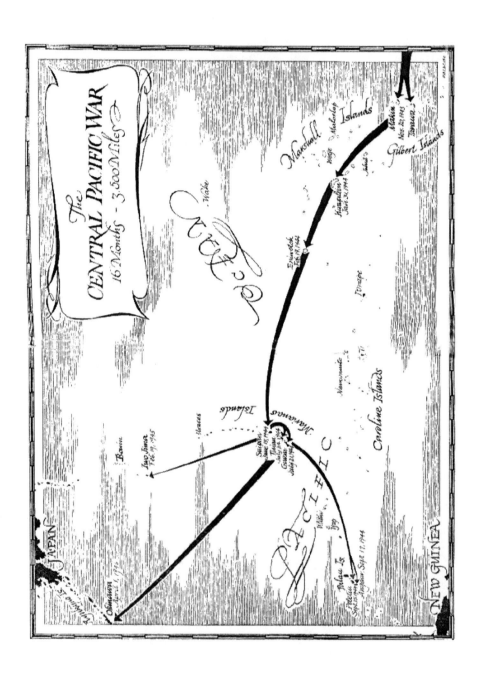

In 1943, the Navy identified this region (map on previous page) as the Central Pacific Area. Except for the Philippines, it would include the vast ocean area north of the Equator as far as the home islands of Japan. Technically, according to world geographers, it was in the North Pacific Ocean, being above the Equator. However, the Navy wanted to differentiate this new offensive from the earlier campaign in the far North Pacific at the Aleutian Islands. Within the next year and a half, United States forces would advance westward 3,500 miles across the Central Pacific from the Gilbert Islands to Okinawa, Japan.

(Written at MCAS EWA)

April 19, 1944

Dear Mother:

Last Sunday morning we were out on a squadron hike. It was already quite hot, being almost noon. As we trudged past the recreation beach, we saw the beer parties going in full swing. There was a large gathering of Seabees. As soon as they saw us, they cheered and ran out to the road, their arms loaded with bottles of beer, which they handed out as our column moved past, saying, "Have some beer, Marine."

Seabees were men of the Navy's construction battalions. Early in 1942, the Navy began recruiting experienced men from the building trades. They were organized into construction battalions to be shipped to far off places for building all types of naval installations, especially airfields. They made their first impact on the American public at Guadalcanal, when, in the late summer of 1942, they toiled alongside the beleaguered Marines to keep Henderson (Air) Field in operation despite regular bombardment from enemy naval and air forces.

Originally, the initials CB or CBs were used in referring to the "construction battalions" themselves. It later developed that the term was applied to the men who made up the battalions. It was those men who turned it into the phrase, "Sea Bees," to draw the parallel with the "busy bees" of the insect family, so adept at constructing geometrically perfect beehives. Being in the Navy, the reference to the "sea" was obvious. The two-word phrase soon became one word, "Seabees." It is a part of our vocabulary today.

(Written at MCAS EWA)

May 2, 1944

Dear Mother:

I saw "Gung Ho" the other night. It didn't come up to my expectations. That excessive Hollywood touch again.

"Lost Angel," which I saw last week, should be one of the top ten for 1944. That little Margaret O'Brien should win an Academy Award. In my opinion, she's on a par with any of the top dramatic actresses on screen.

We have a class in recognition coming up. I guess we can't get too much of that.

---

*   *   *

(Written at MCAS EWA)

May 7, 1944

Dear Mother:

I've been doing considerable thinking on the subject of my education. As you know, during my first two years in college, I majored in Chemistry. Lately, my ideas have been changing on the subject. I think that if I ever go back to college, I'll go more into the social sciences, like sociology, philosophy, psychology, and law.

Mary tells me that there are V-12 Marines at the Mount now. I am going to write Father Cogan and get the dope on it. I'd like to get into V-12 when I get back, and if I worked it right I could get back to the Mount.

(Written at MCAS EWA)

May 12, 1944

Dear Mother:

This will be the last letter you'll receive from me for some time.

We've been attached to the BLANK: Fleet Marine Force. I can't tell you anything, now; but, in time, I'll be able to write and give you the whole story.

---

*   *   *

(Written at MCAS EWA)

> *May 12, 1944*
>
> **Dear Mary:**
>   *This will be just a short note to let you know that you won't hear from me for a long time. I won't have forgotten you. I'll just be too busy with my job, and there won't be any post offices where I'm going.*

On May 12, AWS-5 boarded the *United States Ship Sheridan*, a troop transport numbered PA 61. The acronym, PA, stands for Personnel, Assault. We joined other troops of the Fifth Amphibious Corps and sailed south to the island of Maui. There, we engaged in maneuvers and practice landings, using LCVPs (Landing Craft, Vehicle, Personnel), and the larger LCMs (Landing Craft, Medium). Other troopships that transported Marines in the Pacific were designated APA (Amphibious Personnel, Assault) or KA (Cargo, Assault). Later on, our outfit was transported twice on specialized vessels, called LST (Landing Ship, Tank).

After maneuvers at Maui, our fleet returned to Pearl Harbor in the third week of May 1944. Our *USS Sheridan* tied up in a section of the harbor called West Loch, as did many other troop transports. Some distance away from us, seven LSTs loaded with Marines were moored close together at some pilings about 100 yards out from shore. On the afternoon of May 21, we heard a tremendous explosion in the harbor. We learned later that LST 353 and LST 179 had blown up accidentally, and sank along with at least one other such vessel. The other two or three LSTs were severely damaged.

In a story written some nineteen years later about a hometown Marine who had survived the explosion, the Milwaukee Journal of June 6, 1963, reported that the men lost, including Marines and sailors, had numbered 127 killed and 380 injured.

Back at Pearl Harbor in late May of 1944, other LSTs and Navy crews were brought in, replacing those that were lost. Also, Marine replacements were integrated with survivors so that, within a week, depleted outfits of the Second and Fourth Marine Divisions were brought up to strength and ready to sail.

This incident was not at all publicized during the war because of censorship regulations. The Honolulu newspapers reported merely that there had been fires on some transport ships in the harbor. The Navy conducted an investigation and reached a satisfactory determination that sabotage was not involved; however, no official explanation or report of the incident was released at the time. It became known around the Navy and Marine Corps as the "second disaster at Pearl Harbor."

(Written aboard ship at Pearl Harbor)

May 26, 1944

Dear Mother:
   Yesterday I received your letters of April 14 and 27, and one written April 23 from Dorothy. All three were probably off the same ship, for they were marked with the same receiving date on this side of the ocean.

(Three paragraphs of small talk followed.)

   There's a whole lot that I'd like to tell you, but it'll have to wait until later. When the time comes that I can talk, I'll have enough stored up to write a book about it.

CHAPTER 9

*   *   *

Saipan

On June 1, 1944, my AWS-5 group weighed anchor and departed the Hawaiian Islands, sailing southwest aboard the *Sheridan*. After steaming through the Marshall Islands, our convoy dropped anchor for refueling in Eniwetok Atoll on June 8. This three-islet atoll had been the last and westernmost of the Marshall Islands captured from the Japanese. This had been done four months earlier by the 22nd Marine Regiment and the Army's 105th Infantry Regiment in a three-day battle.

We enjoyed two days diving off the ship and swimming in the cool clear waters of the lagoon. On June 11, we weighed anchor and departed Eniwetok, sailing west. By this time our convoy had grown to more than 600 ships, stretching all around us from horizon to horizon, as far as the eye could see. It would become the largest fleet of the Pacific War up to that time.

We received word aboard ship that we were going to invade a mountainous island called Saipan in the Mariana Islands, the closest landing yet to Japan, 1,500 miles south of Tokyo. By an equivalent distance, we would bypass Rabaul, the Japanese Army's huge South Pacific stronghold in the Bismarck Archipelago, with its 100,000 defenders. We would overshoot, by 700 miles, the vast mid-ocean anchorage for the enemy's Pacific fleet at Truk in the Caroline Islands, just north of the Equator.

The code name for the invasion of Saipan and two other islands in the Marianas was Operation Forager. The planning for the campaign had been done by the officer staff of Fleet Admiral Chester W. Nimitz, Commander in Chief, Pacific Fleet (CINCPAC). His Pacific Fleet Headquarters was located at Makalapa, an extinct volcano, twelve miles outside Honolulu. The name of the volcanic crater means "Flashing Eyes" in Hawaiian.

To avoid confusion in their planning, the staff officers had assigned the usual designation of D-Day to the first scheduled landing at Saipan. Because the other planned landings, at Guam and Tinian, were in the same Operation Forager of the Marianas, a different "day" designation was assigned to each: W-Day would be for Guam, and Jig Day would be for Tinian.

Saipan was twelve miles long, with an average width of four miles. It had a garrison of 30,000 defenders. There was a sizable population of Japanese civilians, plus a few thousand native islanders, called Chamorros.

The plan was for the Second and Fourth Marine Divisions to land side by side on the lower western beaches of the island on June 15, 1944. It would be the first time for two Marine divisions to conduct an amphibious assault together.

In our earlier major landings, only one Marine division at a time had been involved, as follows:

In the Solomon Islands of the South Pacific, the First Marine Division landed at Guadalcanal in 1942. It landed again on New Britain in the Bismarck Archipelago in 1943. The Third Marine Division landed on Bougainville in the Solomons in 1943. In the early atolls of the Central Pacific, the Second Marine Division captured Tarawa of the Gilbert Islands in a ferocious three-day battle in 1943; and the Fourth Marine Division captured Roi-Namur of the Marshall Islands in a less costly three-day battle in February 1944.

Marine Lieutenant General Holland M. Smith commanded the Fifth Amphibious Corps, including the Second and Fourth Marine Divisions and the 27th Infantry Division (Army). Aboard the admiral's flagship, the command ship, *USS Rocky Mount*, at Eniwetok, General Smith, in briefing a group of newsmen, said: "We are through with flat atolls now. We learned how to pulverize atolls, but now we are up against mountains and caves where the Japs can dig in." Then he said slowly, "A week from today there will be a lot of dead Marines."

When Holland M. Smith was a young Marine lieutenant in the Philippine Islands some 35 years earlier, he had urged his platoon to beat the record of another outfit in long-distance, cross-country hiking. To motivate his men, he ranted and raved so much that they called him, "Howlin Mad," instead of Holland M. The nickname stuck throughout his military career.

In preparation for the battle on Saipan, Air Warning Squadron Five (AWS-5), numbering 168 officers and men, had been divided into three sections. I was in the group attached to the 2nd Marine Division. Another group was attached to the 4th Marine Division. A third group was assigned to the 5th Amphibious Corps.

A fully reinforced Marine division numbered about 20,000 men. It consisted principally of three infantry regiments with 3,300 men each. Its one artillery regiment had somewhat fewer men. Each division had seven additional battalions for engineering, tanks, motor transport, medical, and other support services.

In early June 1944, our convoy continued west the next four days, covering some 1,100 miles. On D-Day Minus 2, June 13, our Navy F6F Hellcat fighter planes shot down 124 aircraft from the enemy airfields on Saipan, Tinian, Rota, and Guam in the Marianas, while losing only twelve of their own. The few remaining ships of the Japanese Central Pacific Fleet were sunk or damaged, stranding its commander, Admiral Chuichi Nagumo, at his land-based headquarters on Saipan. Thus, we now had complete air and naval superiority for our landing.

Meanwhile, aboard our transport ships, we continued our daily calisthenics. In addition, we each received a pamphlet containing Japanese words and phrases that might be useful. The only word I remember, to this day, is pronounced: KEY-*OAT*-SKI-*AIY*, meaning ATTENTION! (Italics added for emphasis.) It's a word I had to use once to a group of Japanese prisoners after the battle.

On D-Day, June 15, 1944, our ships arrived off Saipan in the early morning darkness. The ships taking part numbered 775. It was now the largest cross-ocean fleet in history, for the largest amphibious operation of the Pacific War so far.

We were up before dawn and enjoyed the traditional breakfast of steak and eggs for Marines going into battle. At 5:45 a.m., our warships, standing off shore, began firing on the beaches. This armada included three battleships, the *United States Ship Colorado*, and two from the Pearl Harbor attack: the *USS Tennessee*, which had been heavily damaged, and the *USS California*, which had been partially sunk. They, along with cruisers and destroyers, had already been firing on the island for three days before we got there. Now they would lay down an intense barrage for about an hour before the scheduled air strikes.

The infantrymen aboard our ship, with full battle gear, including back packs and rifles, began going over the side of the vessel and down the cargo nets into landing craft at the water below. When loaded, those small vessels moved off to their assigned stations, awaiting their signal to run to the beach, which, for the first waves, would be about two more hours.

At 7 a.m. the heavy bombardment from our warships let up, and the air strikes began. My group was not scheduled to land that morning, so we watched from the railing, as carrier-based Navy war planes peeled off their formations to make bombing and strafing runs at the beaches. This went on for more than an hour. When the air strikes were completed, it was time for the first waves of landing craft to move forward. The signal was given from the commanding vessel, and the assault waves began their runs to the beaches.

Each division sent in two of its regiments to begin landing at H-Hour, set for 8:30 a.m. The Second Division's 6th Marines were assigned as one assault regiment to land the farthest north at Red Beach. Its other regiment, 8th Marines, landed at Green Beach. Further south, below the town of Charan Kanoa, the Fourth Division's two assault regiments, the 23rd and 25th Marines, landed on Blue and Yellow Beaches, respectively. An infantry regiment from each division was held in reserve; each would be landed later on D-Day: the 2nd Marines of the Second Division, and the 24th Marines of the Fourth Division.

The first three waves got ashore and fought inland a few hundred yards against stiff opposition. Then the Japanese artillery opened up to wreak havoc on the succeeding waves as they approached the shore. The amphibious tractors, which had made it safely onto the beach and unloaded troops, then began taking on wounded men to be transported back to the ships.

The total casualties on D-Day, killed and wounded, for both Marine divisions numbered over 2,000. Unfortunately, our two hospital ships were three days late in arriving; so, the troop transports began taking on the wounded. Aboard the *Sheridan,* we took on about 100. We spent all that day comforting the wounded men brought to our ship. Those who died were sent back to the beach to be buried later in the Second Marine Division Cemetery.

On the day after D-Day (D-Plus-1), it was time for my group to go ashore. We went over the railing of the *Sheridan*, down the cargo net, and into the waiting LCVP. As we approached Red Beach, we passed several badly damaged amtracs and various other landing craft foundering in the surf. Others lay stranded on the beach, showing gaping holes from hits by enemy artillery.

The first thing I noticed as I stepped off the LCVP was a row of seven dead Marines. Their bodies, covered with blankets and shelter halves, were lined up on stretchers in the sand. Only their "boondocker"-clad feet were showing. These men had been wounded on D-Day and had been evacuated from the beach at the time. They had succumbed to their wounds aboard transport ships like the *Sheridan*. However, unlike sailors who die aboard ship, they were not to be buried at sea. They were being returned to the island they had fought for. They would be the first bodies interred in a Second Marine Division Cemetery to be started within a few days.

The front line was ahead of us about 400 yards and we heard small-arms fire in the distance. We went through a grove of trees and emerged at a clearing where there was a small landing strip. We took up positions next to an artillery battery beyond the clearing. Ahead of us, the foliated land began to rise up toward 1,550-foot Mount Tapotchau, which occupied the center of the island. There were quite a few dead Japanese soldiers scattered about the field, so we avoided those areas as we dug our two-man foxholes. We noticed one strange Marine picking over those dead bodies to extract gold teeth with a pair of pliers. He dropped his prizes into a little pouch tied to his belt.

At sundown, we ate our K-Rations and settled down in our foxholes for the night. K-Rations consisted of little Cracker-Jack-style boxes, containing meat or eggs, with cheese and biscuits. These could be eaten cold.

We were awakened suddenly, around one o'clock in the morning, by the blasting noise of that artillery battery right next to us. It was firing into the enemy lines and into no-man's land, apparently to deter any advance toward us during the night. Meanwhile, one of our destroyers off shore started lobbing star shells high over the island. These were bright flares that would drift down slowly by parachute to light up the forward terrain. In between rounds fired by the howitzers, I could hear a member of the firing team calling out elevation settings for the gun barrels. This was to mark distance to the target, beginning at around 1,000 yards. The distance became shorter and shorter, until I wondered just how much of no-man's land there might have been left. Then the firing would shift back to the greater distances. This continued through the remainder of the night, and we learned how to get fitful bits of sleep despite the racket.

The next morning, D-Plus-2, after a breakfast of K-Rations, I was ordered to lead my five-man radio team to an observation post on a hilltop overlooking the town of Charan Kanoa. As we headed south along the dusty beach road, I noticed two large groups of native Chamorro women and children, under guard of Marine military police (MPs). The natives were peacefully bathing in the nude at the water's edge along the shore. Further inland we neared the town. We saw a few native women enjoying another bathing session. They were chattering and giggling modestly, as they took turns drawing fresh water from a public well and pouring it over each other.

When we had established our hilltop position, I made radio contact by calling our main base, using "voice procedure" and announcing our call sign. A typical opening might be: *"Keynote One, this is Keynote Two. How do you read me? Over."* Before exchanging information, it was important to advise each other on a scale of one to five how loud and clear we were, such as: *"I read you five by three. How do you read me? Over."* Each operator could then make adjustments in tuning, volume, and things like squelch control, in hopes of achieving radio reception as close to five (loud) by five (clear). Often, we would report the phrase, "loud and clear," when that was the case; otherwise, we would apply the scale of one to five.

It was important for me to use the word "over," so the other operator would know I had released my transmitter button and the airwaves were then free for him to transmit back to me. When it was time to end the exchange, I might have signed off by saying, *"Roger; wilco; out."* This meant: "I *R*eceived your instruction. I *Will c*omply. I'm going *Out* of radio contact." The Morse Code, which we had learned in radio school to be so necessary for fleet operations, was not feasible on the battlefield. The word "Roger" was taken from the phonetic alphabet, which began with Able, Baker, Charlie, Dog.

Incidentally, we could never use the phrase, *"Over and out,"* as we hear sometimes in the old war movies. Those three words, which are mutually exclusive, have somehow caught on. Amateurish movie actors repeat them incessantly, as a tricky phrase, much to my chagrin.

The observation post we used on Saipan was a wooden platform the Japanese had fashioned up high in a large tree. There were open fields all around. The dead bodies of two enemy soldiers, killed on D-Plus-1, lay under the tree. Since we were quite busy getting set up, we didn't take the time to bury them the first day we were there. Meanwhile, we found a small dog in a tree cavity, frightened and cowering from all the artillery noise in the area. We shared our K-Rations with her and she stayed in our camp until the end of the battle.

On June 17, D-Plus-2, the high command realized that Saipan would be tougher than anticipated. The Army's 27th Infantry Division, held in floating reserve, was committed to the battle. The soldiers started landing on the beach near Charan Kanoa. The invasion to recapture Guam, 100 miles south, was postponed. It had been scheduled for the following day. Marine assault forces, standing by aboard ship for Guam, were sent back to the Marshall Islands to await a July landing.

Late on the afternoon of June 17, a company of soldiers from the 27th came ashore and set up camp on the hillside below our outpost. In the evening, I went down the hillside with two other Marines to visit with the soldiers in their camp. We found that their division was made up of men much older than we were, from New York's National Guard. While shooting the breeze, one soldier remarked to me that he and other men in his company did not relish the thought of going into battle. He said that he and many of the soldiers were married and had children at home; that they would rather leave the fighting to us younger and single Marines.

The next morning, D-Plus-3, the soldiers had moved off our hillside toward the flatland below for their assault on Aslito Airfield. The two Marine divisions began attacking north toward Mount Tapotchau and west to Kagman Peninsula, at Magicienne Bay.

From our observation post, we had a great view of the flat, southern end of the island. At the lower end of the island, we could see Aslito Airfield, which the Army division overran without much opposition. Due south, across a three-mile channel, was the island of Tinian, yet to be captured. West of our hill position was Charan Kanoa. General Holland Smith was moving ashore that day, June 18, to set up his Fifth Amphibious Corps headquarters there in a large abandoned house. Straight north was Mt. Tapotchau, where the Japanese forces remained heavily entrenched.

That afternoon we realized that the little dog was beginning to sniff and poke into the bodies of the two dead Japanese soldiers. The corpses had become bloated under the hot sun, were attracting hordes of flies, and were emitting quite a foul stench. So, we buried them a short distance away. We marked the sites by sticking their rifles upright over the graves and placing their helmets on top.

About this time, our three-day supply of K-Rations began to run low. To replenish our food supply, one of our officers dropped off a couple of cardboard cartons containing cans of C-Rations. These were more substantial products of meat and potatoes. They could be heated in our mess kits over small "Sterno" fires. We found C-Rations to be more tasty and filling than the K-Rations; and so did our little dog. By this time, we had named her, "Keynote," after our radio call sign.

On the morning of June 19, D-Day Plus 4, we were surprised to see not a single ship of our huge fleet that had been lying off shore since

D-Day. The Navy had learned from one of our submarines that a potent Japanese task force was on its way from the Philippines to attack our fleet and destroy our beachhead. This forced all of our ships to weigh anchor and vacate the area. Meanwhile, our aircraft carriers sent hundreds of F6F Hellcat fighters forward to intercept over 400 enemy warplanes attacking from the Japanese carriers. That day, 403 enemy planes were shot down in a slaughter, which became known as "the great Marianas turkey shoot." It was the largest single-day record of "kills" made at any time during the war. We had fifty fighter planes shot down in aerial combat. (See F6F Hellcat on Page 104.)

Most of our fighters and torpedo bombers had overspent their fuel supplies and had to return to their carriers after dark. The eleven carriers were the *Bataan, Belleau Wood, Bunker Hill, Cabot, Enterprise, Hornet, Lexington, Monterey, San Jacinto, Wasp, and Yorktown.*

USS Hornet

USS Lexington

In an unprecedented move, contrary to blackout procedures, Task Force 58 Commander Admiral Marc Mitscher won the admiration and gratitude of his pilots by guiding them home with searchlights and deck lights on all of his carriers. Eighty of our planes splashed down in the ocean when they ran out of gas. The next day, when rescue missions could search the waters, many of the aircrews were picked up from their floating life rafts at sea.

On June 21, our fleet returned to Saipan. It was most reassuring to look out from our hillside and see all those ships standing off shore. We needed the transports for our food, water, ammunition, and supplies; the hospital ships for our wounded; the warships for naval gunfire; and the carriers for air support.

After it had overrun Aslito Airfield on D-Plus-3, the Army's 27th Infantry Division began mopping up a small pocket of Japanese holed up in caves on Nafutan Point at the southern tip of the island. After two days, Lieutenant General Holland M. Smith ordered the Army division to take its place in the front line for the Fifth Corps drive north against the main body of Japanese defenders. The 27th moved its division into the attack line between the two Marine divisions facing north. It left behind one battalion of about 1,000 men at Nafutan Point to clean up the enemy stragglers there.

On June 22, we watched as a squadron of Army P-47 Thunderbolt fighter planes began landing at the former Japanese airfield. The airfield's name was now changed from Aslito to Isely Field, in memory of Commander Robert H. Isely, a naval aviator killed during a pre-invasion strike. Also, we could see a battery of 155 howitzers begin firing artillery shells across the three-mile channel at the island of Tinian.

With front-line fighting now having moved well away from our outpost, our daily routine was to report on an occasional enemy airplane that would sneak over from Tinian, or make the longer flight up from Rota, further south. Once the P-47s became operational, the sparse enemy air activity in daylight hours diminished considerably. However, at night we still received occasional bombing runs over Isely Field. The approach of a lone enemy bomber under cover of darkness would be picked by our nearby radar team. My squad would then relay the information by radio to headquarters.

After a day of rest and regrouping, D-Plus-8, June 23, 1944, was set for launching the coordinated attack against the enemy in the drive northward. All three divisions were scheduled to move forward, "jump off," at the same time that morning. As the attack began, it soon became apparent that the Army troops in the center of the line were bogging down, while the Marine divisions on either side were forging ahead. By the end of the day, the Marines on both sides had to circle back to protect their exposed flanks where the soldiers had not advanced in the center.

The senior Army officer on the island at the time was Major General Sanderford Jarman. He was not in charge of any troops involved in the fighting, but was slated to become military governor of the island when the battle was won. He was aware of the situation, and conferred with General Ralph Smith, commander of the Army's 27th Division. The two generals conceded that the 27th was not carrying its full share. General Ralph Smith said that if he couldn't get his division moving forward the following day, he should be relieved of command. The next day, results were no better. The 27th, inexplicably, stayed in place, while the 2nd and 4th Divisions on either side advanced as ordered.

Adm. Raymond A. Spruance, who rose to command the powerful Fifth Fleet

Admiral Raymond Spruance

U.S.S. INDIANAPOLIS   Hoffman Photos, Long Beach, Cal.

Admiral Raymond Spruance (previous page), in charge of the amphibious assault on Saipan, from his command ship, the cruiser, *Indianapolis* (above), reacted to the 27th Division's failure to perform.

He issued an order that its leader, Army Major General Ralph Smith (left), was to be relieved of command.

It fell to Marine Lieutenant General Holland M. Smith (below), commander of

the Fifth Amphibious Corps on shore, to carry out the order. Major General Jarman, the future military governor, took command of the 27th Infantry Division. This incident fomented an Army-Marine controversy back in Hawaii and elsewhere in the Pacific. But that's another story.

The next day, June 25, the 27th Infantry Division began moving forward. With the entire front line advancing, the Fourth Marine Division was able to capture Kagman Peninsula, on the east side of the island. The Second Marine Division fought its way to the summit of 1,550-foot Mount Tapotchau in the center of the island. Thereafter, the three divisions advanced steadily forward, compressing the enemy into the narrow northern portion of the island.

On June 29, two members of AWS-5 were killed in action. Apparently, they were scouting near the front lines in search of a better observation post for air warning. They were Lieutenant Glenn A. Phillips and Corporal Eugene P. Meacci.

Battle scenes on Saipan.

My first letter sent home from Saipan was a short V-Mail note, showing the usual return address of the Fleet Post Office:

(Written at observation post on Saipan)

June 29, 1944

Dear Mother:
This is the first real chance I have had to write you since a month ago.
I am getting along fine, in the best of health. The flies are bad in the day and the mosquitoes at night; but there's no malaria, so we don't worry too much about them. I'm getting a good tan.

All during the battle, Chamorro natives had been coming over to our lines for safety. This was not the case, however, with most Japanese civilians, who believed what their leaders had told them about unspeakable atrocities they would suffer at the hands of the Americans.

In early July the American advance, in the narrow northern sector, pinched out the Second Marine Division. Our front line now had the 27th Infantry Division in the flat land on the western side of Saipan, and the 4th Marine Division in the hilly terrain to the east.

By July 6, General Yoshitsugu Saito and his Japanese forces were bottled up on Marpi Point, at the northern end of the island. He had withdrawn to his sixth and final headquarters cave. He and his staff decided to launch an all-out attack with his remaining troops rather than suffer annihilation from the onslaught of the Americans. He wrote this final order to his troops:

For more than twenty days since the American Devils attacked, the officers, men, and civilian employees of the

Imperial Army and Navy on this island have fought well
and bravely . . . but now we have no materials with which
to fight, and our artillery for attack has been completely
destroyed. Our comrades have fallen, one after another . . . .
The barbarous attack of the enemy is being continued . . .
We are dying without avail under the violent shelling and
bombing. Whether we attack or whether we stay where we
are, there is only death . . . . We must utilize this opportunity
to exalt true Japanese manhood. I will advance with those
who remain to deliver still another blow to the American
Devils, and leave my bones on Saipan as a bulwark of the
Pacific . . . . Here I pray with you for the eternal life of the
Emperor and the welfare of our country, and I advance to
seek the enemy. Follow me!

Actually, General Saito, who had been wounded sometime earlier, was too far-gone in health and strength to lead the attack, so he and his chief of staff committed suicide, called "hara-kiri," that same day. His staff officers cremated the bodies immediately.

The next morning at dawn, 4,000 Japanese soldiers, with some sailors and male civilians, launched the largest banzai attack of the Pacific War. They did not have enough firearms to go around; therefore, many of them carried only knives, machetes, or homemade spears. They swarmed like stampeding cattle against positions defended by the 1st and 2nd Battalions of the Army's 105th Regiment along the flat land of the northwest coast. As their dead and wounded fell in front of them, those behind merely crawled over the bodies and fell into desperate hand-to-hand combat with our soldiers at the front line. The 105th Regiment lost 406 men killed and 512 wounded, but its two front-line battalions accounted for more than 2,000 Japanese dead that morning.

The remaining 2,000 Japanese who broke through the front were mowed down by Marines of the 3rd Battalion, 10th Artillery Regiment. Those gunners, in a rear position to provide artillery support, cut their fuses to four tenths of a second, leveled their 105 howitzers, and fired point blank into the advancing horde. After it was all over, bulldozers were brought up to bury the Japanese bodies in mass graves. An exact count of the enemy dead was impossible, but the burial teams agreed upon a total figure of 4,311 from the banzai charge.

There was another high-ranking Japanese officer on Saipan during the battle, as we learned later. He was Vice Admiral Chuichi Nagumo, (shown here) the once proud commander of the vaunted Japanese carrier fleet that had launched devastating air strikes to attack Pearl Harbor some two years earlier. But now he had no ships and no forces to direct. His recent command had been the Japanese Central Pacific Fleet, but our Navy's pre-invasion air and sea strikes had sunk or damaged what few ships he had remaining. So, the admiral was stranded on Saipan when we landed there three weeks earlier. His few land-locked sailors had been assumed into the defense force by General Saito. The admiral and his aides were relegated to retreat with the general as the Japanese forces were squeezed into the narrow end of the island.

There have been conflicting reports about when Admiral Nagumo committed suicide at the end of the battle of Saipan. There was one report that he may have been seen at least once on the day following the banzai charge. His remains were never found, so we may presume that he also committed hara-kiri and that his aides cremated his body. In any case, the Japanese "hero of Pearl Harbor" came to a rather ignominious end on the tragic island of Saipan one hot July day in 1944.

The day following the banzai charge, July 8, Fourth Division Marines rescued an eight-person team of Catholic Missionaries, originally from Spain. They were found in a cave in the northeast corner of the island, where they had been held under guard by Japanese military police. All of them had spent many years as missionaries on the island. They included a Jesuit priest, his assistant, and six Sisters of Mercy.

Later that day, organized resistance ended on the island and it was declared secured the following day, July 9.

During the next two days, there followed the most bizarre and pathetic episode yet encountered during our offensive across the Central Pacific. At the northern end of the island, hundreds of Japanese civilians, some being forced by their own soldiers, waded into the surf and drowned themselves, or jumped to their deaths off the high cliffs. Others gathered in small groups to blow themselves up with grenades. All of this was in spite of our efforts to reassure their safety. We had interpreters and some of our Japanese prisoners plead with them over loudspeakers not to kill themselves and to come over to our lines.

We learned later that newsreel scenes of the suicides, which were played up in movie theaters back home, had shocked the American public. However, not shown in equal time were the hundreds of civilians who did respond to our appeals and were filmed streaming into our lines. So, unfortunately, the impression was made back home that practically the whole civilian population had perished in the battle. In fact, our internment camps registered around 15,000 civilians, both Japanese and Chamorro. I didn't hear of any Chamorro natives who committed suicide.

On July 10, the day after the island was declared secured, over 2,000 Japanese soldiers were killed by Marines during mopping up operations. The Second Division was credited with 508 enemy soldiers that day, and the Fourth Division with some 1,500 more.

The military casualties on Saipan were the most numerous of the Pacific war up to that time. Of the 30,000-man Japanese garrison, 1,734 were taken prisoner, including 236 wounded. An estimated 27,500 enemy soldiers were killed in action. For a year after the battle, Army garrison forces rounded up several hundred more enemy stragglers. There were 3,659 Americans killed on land during the three-and-one-half-week battle of Saipan; 12,866 were wounded.

In Japan, Fleet Admiral Osami Nagano, supreme naval advisor to the Emperor, lamented, "Hell is upon us."

Emperor Hirohito of Japan

Prime Minister Hideki Tojo was forced to resign.

Hideki Tojo

F6F Hellcat, featured in "the great Marianas turkey shoot," mentioned on Page 93.

CHAPTER 10

* * *

After the Battle on Saipan and at Sea

When the battle ended, I led my squad down off the hilltop into the town of Charan Kanoa. There we camped out in an abandoned house, along with other members of AWS-5. The remaining letters I wrote home from Saipan were all from that location. They are quoted, in part, as follows:

(Written at Charan Kanoa on Saipan)

July 10, 1944

Dear Mother and Mary:

This island has been secured and all organized resistance has ended. At ten o'clock this morning the American flag was raised. I went over to watch the proceedings, perching myself up on the roof of a shed. A Marine newsreel photographer followed suit and joined me on the roof. He then proceeded to use me as his "tripod," as he filmed the ceremony with his camera.

> *There were generals, a few admirals, a whole slew of colonels, and numerous other officers on down the line. There was quite a large gathering of Marines on hand for the occasion, with a few sailors and soldiers scattered here and there.*
>
> *While I was up in the hills at my outpost, I adopted a really cute female dog. When I found her she was frightened and hungry. It didn't take her long to get over that though, when she realized we were going to take care of her and feed her. We decided to call her Keynote—Keynote, being the call sign of our radio outpost. She really took to her name, and the Skipper says she'll be an asset to the squadron.*

Two days later I sent a letter to my older sister, Dorothy, who was at the seminary in Emmitsburg. In this case, it probably went through a different censoring officer, for the part about Keynote and our call sign was cut out.

(Written on Saipan)

> *July 12, 1944*
>
> *Dear Dottie:*
>
> *The battle here is over. It was a bad time while it was going on. Now, we can't wait to get off the island. Our work here is done and the Army garrison force is taking over, so we won't be here too much longer.*
>
> *There are some things I'm going to try to get cleared tomorrow so that I can take them off the island. One thing that I think will be of interest to you is a series of work sheets which the native children here have used to learn English. I imagine it was taught in missionary schools.*

Regarding missionary people on the island, there was a party of two priests and six nuns rescued by the Marines about a week ago during the final push against the enemy.

I have adopted a cute little female dog for a pet. She's really

 *taken to me in a big way. We named her* **BLANK:** *Keynote, after the radio call sign we had up in the hills.*

I'll be able to tell you loads of stories about the country, the people, the towns, etc., when I get back.

*   *   *

(V-Mail to Sister Leo, St. Joseph's College)

July 20, 1944

(V-Mail was a special one-page letter used in World War Two. See next page.)

Dear Dorothy:

We are still here on Saipan, waiting to get off.

I've gotten some metal (duraluminum) from a wrecked Japanese airplane. I'm going to fashion some wrist bracelets. Mary would like one, but I haven't told her yet. Lately I've been working on a telephone-wire, salvage detail. We have three

> *native Chamorros working with us: Francisco, Prudentio, and*
> *Jose. They are very happy to be working for Uncle Sam and*
> *making more money than ever in their lives. They talk a lot*
> *about the Padres and Madres.* (They were referring to their
> priests and sisters. FVG, 1995) *Most of them wear the rosary*
> *around their necks.*

On July 21, the Third Marine Division and the First Marine Provisional Brigade invaded Guam, 100 miles south of Saipan, in the Marianas. The planners of Operation Forager had labeled the day scheduled for landing as W-Day. I suppose the W stood for War. On the following day, the Army's 77th Infantry Division went ashore on Guam and joined in the battle. That former American territorial island, twice as large as Saipan, was defended by two thirds as many men. It was liberated from Japanese rule in a month-long battle.

The following letter is printed out of chronological order because of format configuration.

(Written on Saipan)
(V-Mail to Ensign M. B. Gardner, USNR)

> *July 15, 1944*
>
> *The official word came through today that*
> *we are now allowed to divulge the name of this*
> *island we've been fighting for. As you have*
> *probably already gathered, the name of this*
> *place is Saipan.*
> *We are all ready and waiting, and will shove*
> *off any day now.*

> *The most annoying thing about this island now is the heavy rainfall; and when we first came in, it was the dust.*

(The advantage of V-Mail was that hundreds of one-page messages could be photographed overseas, placed on microfilm, sent to the United States for enlargements, folded into window envelopes, then mailed free to their final destinations.)

(Written on Saipan)

July 22, 1944

Dear Mother:

Today I was down at the Chamorro camp. A buddy of mine from aboard ship, who is in the Naval Civil Affairs Committee, had me admitted to the compound. There were six nuns of the Order of Mercy. They are conducting a school for the little Chamorro children. Their home was Spain, which they left 10 and 18 years ago. I told them about Dorothy and of your thirst for the Spanish language. They are from the northern part of Spain.

I was thinking that it might help you with your lessons to have a correspondence with them. The Spanish class would enjoy it; historical value, too. I'll work on it.

While our outfit was waiting to leave the island, we were assigned to a work detail, salvaging miles of telephone wire. This involved climbing palm trees or telephone poles to detach the wires that had been strung up hastily during the battle. In our outfit, we had experienced telephone men who taught us the proper way to climb, using both hands and feet. Around our legs we strapped metal brackets that held sharp spikes pointed down and inward at the bottom. We climbed the poles or trees by angling our feet against the wood so the spikes dug in. When we stopped to rest, or to use our hands in detaching the wire, we would secure a heavy belt around the pole or tree to keep from falling.

(Left to right, standing) Frank Gardner, Pete, and Serache; (kneeling) Gordon and Mulhearn. (Other full names not available.)

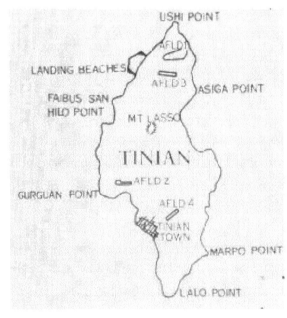

On July 24, the Fourth Marine Division invaded the island of Tinian, using only landing craft, across the three-mile channel from Saipan. The Second Division landed the following day. I was not involved in this operation. It was the only major shore-to-shore amphibious assault in the Central Pacific. Earlier in the war, the Marines had employed such tactics on a smaller scale in the Solomon Islands of the South Pacific.

The landing on Tinian was referred to as Jig Day. Jig was taken from the phonetic alphabet's lineup: "Item, Jig, King, etc." Thus, the officers of Makalapa, in planning for the three landings of Operation Forager in the Marianas, would be dealing with only one actual D-Day, on the first landing at Saipan. The other two landings would each use a different letter of the alphabet to avoid confusion.

Tinian, a flat island a bit smaller than Saipan and defended by a third as many men, was secured in a quick one-week battle.

With the acquisition of the three largest and most important islands in the Marianas, our Armed Forces began preparing five airfields for long-range bombing of Japan by the vaunted B-29 Superfortresses.

After having met the sisters mentioned in my July 22 letter, I visited them for about a week at their compound on Saipan every afternoon at the end of our daily salvage work. They were housed in wooden barracks built by the Seabees. The first day at the compound, I had tromped into their building, oblivious to the array of shoes and sandals on the wooden staircase outside. Inside, I soon became aware that the sisters were in their stocking feet. So, I quickly excused myself, went outside, and added my "boondocker" shoes to the line-up on the stairs.

*　　*　　*

Frank Gardner (center), with Keynote, flanked by Seabourne (left) and Duffy (right), both holding puppies. Behind Seabourne is George Izquierdo in the white shirt. Next

to Duffy (holding weapon) is Milton Urban, from El Paso, Texas. Other members of AWS-5 are gathered around after the Battle of Saipan, July 1944, Charan Kanoa.

*   *   *

The Mother Superior, Sister Angelica Saliverria, spoke limited English, but we struggled through our first enjoyable meeting. (Italics shown to emphasize pronunciation.) She indicated that the native Chamorros were most grateful to us for liberating them from Japanese rule, and now they wanted to be protected by the United States.

Sister said she would like to learn our National Anthem so she could teach it to the children at her missionary school. I wrote down the words in English. As I sang the lines, one of the sisters picked out the musical notes on her guitar. Over the next two days they practiced the anthem with me. Then they taught it to the children.

> Oh, say can you see by the dawn's early light
>> What so proudly we hailed at the twilight's last gleaming?
> Whose broad stripes and bright stars, through the perilous fight
>> O'er the ramparts we watched, were so gallantly gleaming?

One day, on my way to visit the sisters at the Chamorro compound, I lost track of Keynote. Apparently, some of the natives camped along the road had lured her into one of their huts nearby. After searching the area and not finding her, I was reconciled that at least she would have a home on her own island.

On the morning of July 27, Sister Angelica asked me to come and hear the children sing. They had a ceremony in the center of the Chamorro compound, where their people gathered around and raised the American Flag. Then, those little native schoolchildren, their shiny faces beaming, sang the song the sisters had taught them, our National Anthem.

And the rocket's red glare, the bombs bursting in air,
    Gave proof through the night that our flag was still there!
Oh, say does that Star Spangled Banner yet wave
    O'er the land of the free, and the home of the brave?

When I first met Sister Angelica Saliverria on Saipan, I was aware that she had suffered some kind of injury during the battle. Since the wound was covered by her clothing, she passed it off as nothing important. Many years later, when I read a letter she had sent to my mother, I learned it was actually a bullet wound. (See Page 190.)

The fourth nun on the right is Sister Angelica Salaverria. The sisters are surrounded by Chamorros at Internment Camp, attending Catholic mass after the Battle of Saipan. Marine Captain John M. Popham is in the foreground.

Witnessing that ceremony brought a huge lump to my throat and a little tear to my eye. On that occasion I had to bid farewell to my new friends, for our outfit was shoving off that afternoon. So, I was able to leave that tragic island with some small sense of accomplishment; I had touched some gentle people and made a little difference.

Since we were the first ground troops to depart the Marianas, Air Warning Squadron Five was given the assignment of standing guard over prisoners of war being evacuated from the island. The enemy troops captured on Saipan numbered 1,734. Of these, 1,498 were being shipped to prisoner-of-war camps in Hawaii. The remaining 234 had been wounded; they were still being treated on the island.

There would be about 500 prisoners on each of three ships. One third of our squadron, about 55 Marines each, was assigned to guard each contingent. Those of us who had landed on Saipan with the Second Marine Division were assigned to guard 500 Japanese prisoners aboard the *USS J. Franklin Bell.*

On the afternoon of July 27, we went over to the prison compound and picked up our 500 prisoners. We formed them up outside the camp, and marched them down toward the beach, amid much noise and dust. Groups of native Chamorros gathered alongside the road to gawk at our strange procession.

This proved to be a momentous event, not only for those curious Chamorros, but also for one little dog that was also attracted to the hustle and bustle. It was Keynote! She recognized our Marines, in their dungarees and camouflaged helmet covers, marching alongside the formation of prisoners. She broke away from a group of natives and began running up and down the column. When my buddies saw her and called her by name, she started running back toward my direction. When I saw her, I gave a loud six-note whistle, which she knew immediately as her special call. It consisted of the musical notes: C, D, C, B, C, and high C. She came running to my side and we greeted each other with much excitement. She didn't leave my side again as we departed Saipan that day.

*   *   *

Marines, who went back to Saipan for the 50th Anniversary, in June of 1994, report that there are some notable changes on the island. Near the beaches where we landed in 1944 there is a McDonald's hamburger stand and a Kentucky Fried Chicken outlet. Modern hotels, including a few that are quite luxurious, are scattered from north to south along the western coast of the island. They go from the small city we knew as Garapan to the town of Charan Kanoa, where the sugar refinery used to be. That town called Charan Kanoa, where General "Howlin Mad" Smith had his Fifth Amphibious Corps headquarters and where we camped after the battle ended, has been renamed Chalan Kanoa. Aslito Airfield, later named Isely Field, is now called Saipan International Airport. There is an American Memorial Park at Tanapag.

Following the war, the Mariana Islands north of Guam, principally Saipan, Tinian, and Rota, were held for more than 30 years by the United States as a Trust Territory. In 1975 the inhabitants held a plebiscite in which 78.8 per cent of them voted for their islands to become an American Commonwealth. In 1981 they became an American possession, called the Commonwealth of the Northern Marianas. Guam, the southernmost island in the Marianas, was not included in this arrangement, retaining its original status as a United States Territory.

Every year, thousands of Japanese tourists still visit Saipan, where they pay homage at the Suicide Cliff, Banzai Cliffs, and the Last Command Post of General Saito.

Most of the 2,600 Marines and 1,000 soldiers killed on Saipan in 1944 remain buried there in the three division cemeteries. In a few cases, however, when, after the war, some of the families had so requested, bodies were disinterred and returned home for reburial.

*   *   *

Down at the beach that July afternoon of 1944, we loaded our prisoners aboard landing craft, and took them out to our ship, the *J. Franklin Bell* (PA 16) in Tanapag Harbor. There were twenty Japanese officers in the group, who were lodged in a forward compartment at the bow. The 480 enlisted men were housed amidships down in the deep cargo hold, where they were to sleep on stanchion cots stacked four tiers high.

Our first day aboard ship, I was in charge of the detail on guard duty down in the hold. The first order of business for the prisoners was sanitation. Under the direction of our second lieutenant, Luther A. Reedy, all the prisoners were deloused with a white, powdery spray. Then, with their top sergeant gleefully ordering them to line up, each one had his head shaved. When the last one had gone through this procedure, Lt. Reedy then told the unsuspecting top sergeant that it was his turn. The man's carefree demeanor turned to one of dismay, as he sat for his haircut to the tune of friendly jeers and catcalls from his own men.

The first meal served to the prisoners consisted of chicken a la king on rice. A prison detail brought down two large, brand new "G.I." cans from the galley. One was loaded down with chicken, and the other with rice. Each man was given a bowl and spoon for eating his allotted portion of food. When all had been served, a Japanese sergeant came up to me, indicating that the serving detail was ready to carry the food back to the galley. I checked the "G.I." cans and saw that there was still plenty of unused food left in them. So I told the sergeant they ought to finish it up. Apparently, the sergeant had not expected this, and when he understood what I meant, he seemed surprised, but pleased. He then announced that second helpings were available, and many lined up immediately, grinning and gesticulating, since they could not suppress their happiness.

Later that evening I was expecting our commanding officer, Captain Donald D. O'Neill, to escort his Japanese counterpart down to the hold for an inspection tour. When I saw them approaching down the ladder, I remembered the Japanese word for "attention" we had studied before the battle. So, I shouted out, KEY *OAT* SKI *AIY*! Immediately, every prisoner jumped to his feet and stood stiffly at attention as the officers inspected them and their quarters.

We got under way the next morning, July 28, 1944, as our *J. Franklin Bell,* and the other two ships weighed anchor from Tanapag Harbor. One of the other ships was loaded with 500 Korean laborers, who had been pressed into service by the Japanese Army for building fortifications on Saipan. Because they were uniformed members of the army, although in a second class status as laborers, we had to count them as prisoners of war and treat them as such.

The third ship in our little convoy was loaded half with Japanese and half with Korean prisoners. This mixture, we were told later, caused a lot of trouble aboard that ship. The enmity and friction between those two groups, who did not like each other, erupted several times in confrontations and a few fist fights or wrestling encounters. Conversely, on our ship, with its well-disciplined Japanese troops, and on the other ship filled with the rather docile Koreans, there was no trouble at all.

In the hold of our ship, most of the prisoners were quartered down in the lower section, while fewer men were scattered around a middle-deck landing. From that landing down to the bottom of the hold, a very wide and long, temporary staircase, without the usual hand railings, had been installed. On board ship, we used the Navy's term "ladder" for stairs and staircases.

On the second day out, with gently rolling seas, I was on guard duty. I had seated myself on the landing, with my feet planted on the top step of the wide ladder. I held my rifle in the "rest" position in front of me.

One of the prisoners was mounting the ladder. Suddenly, the ship lurched sharply to one side and the prisoner was thrown off balance. Instinctively, he reached out and grabbed the barrel of my rifle so as not to fall backwards down the ladder. When he realized what he had done, he dropped to his knees and pleaded for mercy, apparently thinking I might strike him for his untoward action. I reached out, took his hand, and helped him to his feet and onto the landing. I reassured him that everything was all right. He bowed and thanked me profusely, obviously very much relieved.

One day, a prisoner named Watanabe and some others were asking us where they were going. We knew we were going back to Pearl Harbor, but we couldn't tell them that. They indicated that they really hoped they would go to California, which they had heard so much about and had seen so much of in the movies from Hollywood. Again, we stopped at Eniwetok for refueling, this time for two days.

Two Japanese prisoners, who had been sickly, died aboard our ship during the two-week voyage back to Hawaii. I participated in one of the burial ceremonies. A weight was tied to the body so it would not float. The remains were completely wrapped up, covered by a Japanese flag, and placed on a flat board at the railing of the ship.

Several groups gathered at the railing for the ceremony. They were: U. S. Navy officers from the *J. Franklin Bell;* a platoon of sailors from the ship's company; officers of AWS-5; a platoon of our Marines; three Japanese officers; a group of prisoners as pallbearers; and my squad to fire a rifle salute. A Japanese officer said some Shinto prayers over the deceased; my squad fired three volleys over the railing; the pallbearers tilted the platform; and the body slipped beneath the Japanese flag into the ocean.

On August 10, 1944, we docked at Pearl Harbor. We said a friendly good-bye to Watanabe and the others as they filed down the gangplank. From there, Army MPs took them off to a prison camp. We of AWS-5 went back to our old barracks at the Ewa Marine Corps Air Station.

(Written at MCAS EWA)

> *Sgt. F. V. Gardner, USMC*
> *AWS-5 Marine Assault*
> *Fleet Post Office*
> *San Francisco, California*
> *August 14, 1944*
>
> *Dear Mother:*
> *We are back at our rear base now. We enjoyed the trip back, having only a hold full of Japanese prisoners of war to guard. Being the only troops aboard, we were not held to the usual crew-and-troop distinction by the sailors.*
> *You will notice that the "Air Transportable" in our address has been changed to Marine Assault.*
> *The chow on board was the best yet, and there were movies every night in the sweatbox they called the forward mess hall.*
> *Forget about Fred and those other names on the list I sent back in January. I lost their names anyway.* (My reference to "Fred" was to let mother know I would not make any further efforts to apply my ineffective "whereabouts code.")

While at Ewa, I went to a military supply store and bought some Second Marine Division shoulder patches, which I sewed on my khaki shirts. The patch is in the shape of a spearhead, the center of which displays a hand-held flaming torch with a large number "2." This is surrounded by a constellation of stars, depicting the Southern Cross, on a field of red. I wore the patch proudly to demonstrate the division I had been attached to in combat. The Second Marine Division patch is on display in my den at home.

The Second Division was the only Marine unit that earned a battle star on each of five different Pacific islands in World War Two. They were Guadalcanal, Tarawa, Saipan, Tinian, and Okinawa.

(Written at MCAS EWA)

August 17, 1944

Dear Mother:

Today I received a batch of back mail, all dated in May and June. Those letters followed me to Saipan and back. Now I'm beginning to understand and piece together some of the things you said in your later letters, which came directly here.

Right now the radio is playing selections from Pinafore, such as, "Poor Little Buttercup" and "Now He is the Ruler of the Queen's Nighvy." Also, that one where he sings, "What, never?" Then, the chorus replies, "No, never!"

Let's see now, I have about a dozen of your letters to answer, and some of Mary's. I'll have to answer hers in a separate letter.

Use your discretion about sending more books. As for me, we have plenty of books in Station and Ship Libraries. When these are not available, it means we're too busy for books anyway. Coming back aboard ship, I managed to read two books by Van Wick Mason: "Three Harbours" and "The Fighting American." I like Mason as an author.

Enclosed you will find a 5 yen note I found on the island. Their 5 yen is equal to one American dollar.

CHAPTER 11

$*$ $*$ $*$

Rest and Reorganization on Oahu

Because we had just returned from combat, our squadron, AWS-5, was scheduled for some rest and rehabilitation. Some of our men were feted for three days at the famous Royal Hawaiian Hotel on Waikiki Beach in Honolulu. However, before my turn came up, we had to undergo some training exercises, and the remainder of us never made it to the hotel. When I wrote home about this, being hampered by censorship restrictions, I couldn't divulge the name or location of the place.

My next letter home was to my older sister, Dorothy. By this time, she had finished her seminary training and had received the habit as a Daughter of Charity. She took the name of Leo, in honor of our Aunt Leo, her favorite aunt. As a small child, Dorothy had spent two years with Aunt Leo and Uncle Lud on their farm in the Mount Vernon District of Fairfax County, Virginia.

(Written at MCAS EWA, Oahu, T.H.)

August 18, 1944

My dear Sister Leo:

Well, we're now back here at our rear base again. It's really good to be here, enjoying this rest period.

On the way back we did a lot of guard duty over Japanese prisoners of war. I was down in the hot, smelly hold of the ship for long periods at a time. This caused much of my tan to wash off with perspiration.

About those sheets and books I mentioned to you, I'm going to include them in a large package to mother, and she can pass them on to you. I have a few Japanese notes I'll send you in my next letter.

* * *

(Written at MCAS EWA)

August 21, 1944

Dear Mother:

The little excursion I was to go on didn't materialize. The deal was that we were to go to a famous hotel for a three-day rest. The hotel is a former civilian one that has been taken over by the Navy. It fell through at the last minute for some of us, but we're still hoping to get in on it.

* * *

(Written at MCAS EWA)

August 21, 1944

Dear Mary:

    Yes, bread certainly was a luxury on Saipan. During the whole time I was there, I ate only two slices. There were a few isolated cases when we could beg, borrow, or steal it from the Army.

    Well, I've started my old swimming routine again. Boy, I certainly am out of shape. I hope we stay here a while so I can get my speed back. I've lost some of my wind; I can tell by my underwater swimming.

About this time, Sister Angelica Salaverria on Saipan wrote a letter to mother in Spanish. Apparently, because of language difficulty, she misspelled mother's first and last names, which resulted in some delay in the letter being delivered.

The letter opens in the first paragraph in Spanish, as follows:

    Soy una Mercedaria Misionera espanola que estoy aqui en Saipan hace nueve anos. Hace dos o tres semanas tuve el gusto de conocer a su buenisimo hijo Francis que nos hiso pasar un rato muy agradable.

Thirty-five years later, after I had learned the Spanish language in the Foreign Service, I was able to translate most of the letter. A friend, Stephanie Van Reigersberg, a linguist at the Department of State, assisted me in the more complicated passages.

Catholic Mission
Saipan, Mariana Islands
August 25, 1944

Ensign Maria B. Garner, U.S.N.R. (Marie B. Gardner)
1020 19th Street, N, W,
Washington, 6 D. C.

Dear Madam:

I am a missionary sister of Mercy from Spain who has been here on Saipan for the past nine years. Two or three weeks ago I had the pleasure of meeting your fine son, Francis, with whom we had a very pleasant visit. He asked me to write you and I am delighted to do so because I know how much it means to a mother to hear news of a son who is far away and in danger. I saw him, as I say, healthy of body; but, what is more comforting to you, he seemed to me healthy and good of soul. You can thank God for giving you such a fine son. I pray to the Lord to preserve his life and to give you the comfort of seeing him again after the war.

He told me you know some Spanish Carmelites. From which Province in Spain are they?

We have suffered a lot from the war, but now, thanks be to God, we are doing quite well because the Americans are treating us with much affection and have given us everything we need.

Do not forget this missionary sister in your prayers, and I will not forget you in mine.

Angelica Salaverria
Missionary Sister of Mercy

I spent the last week of August at the rifle range on Oahu. On September 2, the last day on the range, I fired a score of 310 qualifying as a rifle expert.

(Written at MCAS EWA, Oahu, T. H.)

September 2, 1944

Dear Mother and Mary:

Well, I've been out at the rifle range all week and am now back at the base for one night before shoving off again for another week. At the range I fired expert. Remember, two years ago I fired sharpshooter.

Next week I will be away at Jungle Training and Survival School. It ought to be interesting.

Yes, those six nuns I visited on Saipan are the same ones you read about being rescued during the battle. Right now I'm trying to get an address by which I can send some money and stamps to them.

As for your question on our chaplain, our outfit doesn't have one. We're too small. So, we just adopt the chaplain of any larger outfit we're attached to or ship we're loaded on. Enclosed is a picture of the priest who was the Navy chaplain on our troop transport going to Saipan. He was around age 50, with white hair, and a fine man, as I remember him. He worked relentlessly among the wounded and dying Marines brought aboard our ship on D-Day.

Enclosed is a picture** of our group taken in Charan Kanoa after the island was secured. The dogs are, from left to right: "Airborne," who stayed on the island; "Keynote," held by me; and "Saipan."

** The photo is shown earlier in this book, on Page 111.

On September 2, 1944, the U. S. Navy aircraft carrier *San Jacinto* sent its planes to bomb Chichi Jima in the Bonin Islands, about 600 miles south of Tokyo, Japan. The two most important islands there were Chichi Jima, a major radio communications base, and Iwo Jima, an important air base. The purpose of the raid was to make a quick strike to damage and disrupt the communications center at Chichi, while avoiding retaliatiu from enemy fighter planes at the Iwo air base, 100 miles south.

During the attack on Chichi Jima, an *Avenger* torpedo bomber piloted by Lieutenant George Herbert Walker Bush was shot down. He parachuted safely into the ocean, but his two gunner crewmen were lost. The submarine USS Finback rescued the pilot from his life raft three miles off Chichi Jima. He survived the war and went on to become the 41st president of the United States, President George Bush.

Eleven of our fliers who were shot down and captured at Chichi Jima during the war did not survive. Investigators learned after the war that some were beheaded and eaten by six Japanese officers on the island. After the war, in 1947, those treacherous offenders were hanged for their cannibalistic behavior.

(Written at MCAS EWA)

September 10, 1944

Dear Mother:
  Well, I've just finished a week of intensified "jungle training." As at the rifle range, we were kept very busy, which explains my neglect in writing. We took Keynote and Saipan out there with us, and they fared very well the whole time.

(These were the two dogs we brought from the island of Saipan.)

On September 15, 1944, the First Marine Division invaded Peleliu in the Palau Islands, Central Pacific. Marine casualties amounted to

1,241 killed, and 5,024 wounded. The Army's 321st Infantry Regiment reinforced the Marines on September 23. The soldiers suffered 277 men killed, and 1,008 wounded. About 10,000 enemy soldiers were killed, and 302 were taken prisoner in a two-month battle.

(Written at MCAS EWA)

September 16, 1944

Dear Mother:

We're now on a good schedule of drill, exercise, and instruction. Also, I've started training with the base swimming team. It's only six days since I started, and already I can notice a big change. I'm feeling better all around and my speed has picked up too. It'll be two or three weeks before I'm ready to swim in a meet.

A few days later, I went Christmas shopping in Honolulu, Hawaii, to find a present for my sister, Mary. I described it to Dorothy in the following letter.

(Written at MCAS EWA)

September 20, 1944

Dear Dottie:

The other day I was on liberty. I spent practically the whole time trying to find a good Christmas present for Mary. I searched every jewelry store and gift shop in town and was about to give up when I passed a dress shop. The idea hit me like a light: an evening gown! So, I went in and bought the best they had in size 14. Was I right in the size?

> *I know that she certainly can use one, with all those dances coming up at the Mount. I'm going to send it this week. It'll be an early Christmas present, but she'll be able to use it this fall.*

*   *   *

(Written at MCAS EWA)

October 4, 1944

Dear Mother;

 Last night we swam in a triangular meet with the Navy and the Seabees. We won. Enclosed is a picture of the team. We are the champions of the island.

(I am shown seated at the far right.)

*   *   *

(Written at MCAS EWA)

October 8, 1944

Dear Mother:

 A while back I told you that I was sending some papers and some Japanese literature home. The package is being held up for clearance by intelligence.

In mid-October, I, along with a few other radio operators from AWS-5, went to study at a Navy radar training school on Oahu. The idea was that in some future battle we might have to be pressed into service to operate the radar equipment as well as our radios. It turned out to be a training exercise that we radio operators would never need. Unknown to us at the time, the need for our type of air warning unit was already under review. We would learn shortly that our outfit was to be discontinued.

(Written at Navy Radar School, Oahu, T. H.)

October 17, 1944

Dear Mother:

You probably noticed the return address on the envelope. It was necessary to use it while I am here at this school. But I'll be here only a very short time. So, please disregard it and use my old address.

We have Keynote and Saipan here with us. They don't get along too well here in this Navy camp, especially Keynote. Earlier, I told you that she didn't go for sailors? She's getting used to them, though; for they usually wear blue dungarees. However, every once in a while a gob in whites will arouse her a bit. Our puppy, Saipan, is about as tall as Keynote now. His legs are longer, but she's still heavier.

Sometime soon I should be promoted to staff sergeant. The promotion list went in a little while ago, before we were assigned to this school. So, when and if the rate comes through, it won't be because of anything gained in this Radar Operators School. It'll be more from my work on Saipan.

One day at the Navy radar school, a black sailor in white uniform tried to make a short cut through the front yard of our Marine Quonset hut. Keynote jumped up and started barking at him. He kicked her and she kept barking even more. I intervened immediately to call her off and to explain to the sailor that she was merely protecting our territory. The sailor, who was a cook in the base galley, retorted that it was more Navy territory than Marine. A shouting match then developed between the huge, 300-pound sailor, on one hand, and my buddies and me on the other.

The sailor said he would not leave our front yard unless we agreed to a boxing match. I ended that standoff by agreeing to meet him in the ring. About two days later the sailor and I met in the boxing ring. A few Marines and about two hundred sailors gathered around to cheer us on.

Boxing was a big thing in the Navy. Every ship and every naval base had its boxing ring, and many disputes among shipmates were settled there.

We each wore boxing gloves and had our own handlers in our corner for the occasion. There was a referee, a three-minute bell, and three rounds of hit and run. He could hit very hard, but he couldn't move too fast. If I got too close he could really knock me around. So, I hit fast and ran fast. He hurt me a lot more than I hurt him, but it ended up as a draw. For the many sailors and few Marines, it was something they could all cheer about. The sailor and I shook hands at the end and there were no hard feelings left, except for my fat lip and a few other bruises. My buddies congratulated me for putting up a good fight.

The only blacks in the Navy at the time were cooks, bakers, and stewards for the officers' mess. When I enlisted back in 1942, there were no black Marines. Around 1944, the Marine Corps began accepting blacks who had been drafted, and they were placed in segregated units for transportation and supply services. So far, I had not seen any.

*   *   *

In the extended Southwest Pacific Area, on October 20, 1944, General Douglas MacArthur returned to the Philippines. He directed the U. S. Sixth Army, commanded by Lieutenant General Walter Krueger, to land that morning on a 17-mile front along the coast of Leyte. Four infantry divisions landed about four miles apart between Dulag and Tacloban, meeting little resistance. The Japanese were caught unprepared on shore. The only defending troops there at the time, the Japanese 16th Division, withdrew quickly to the northwest section of the island.

In the early afternoon of that day, with newsreel cameras and photographers recording the dramatic event, General MacArthur waded ashore with his entourage. Within the hour the general stepped before a battery of microphones hastily set up on the beach. With the assembled press corps watching and filming, he announced in a radio message to the Philippine people, "I have returned."

(Written at Navy Radar School, Oahu, T. H.)

October 23, 1944

Dear Mother:

Everything's going along fine here in school. I'm getting that package cleared now. You ought to be getting it in due time.

---

*   *   *

(Written at Navy Radar School, Oahu)

October 28, 1944

Dear Dottie:

Those Japanese worksheets are already on their way. I just mailed them the other day. You see, I spent a lot of time getting to a place where I could get them cleared. The Naval Intelligence office here at this school got things done in short order. The package is going to mother. She'll forward the worksheets to you. Also, there are some textbooks, which she'll probably keep herself. There's one book that ought to prove interesting to your 7th and 8th grade science pupils.

*   *   *

(Written at Navy Radar School, Oahu)

October 31, 1944

Dear Mother:

I'll have a whole lot to tell you when I get back; but it'll have to be person to person. You see, none of it can go through the mail. The censorship regulations are very strict. So, in our writing we make it a practice to shy away from talking shop for fear that the letter will be returned by the censor. Then I'd have to write another letter in which about all I could say would be: "I'm fine. Keynote's fine. How are you?" It's very difficult to write a letter when you can't even mention the (Shhh) w-e-a-t-h-e-r.

---

*   *   *

(Written at Navy Radar School, Oahu)

November 9, 1944

Dear Mother:

As of tomorrow, the 169th anniversary of the Marine Corps, and three months to the day since we got back from Saipan, there will no longer be a Marine Assault AWS-5. We are being broken up. I'll give you all the gruesome details when I get back to the base. That will be very shortly because we're finishing up our courses here at radar school in jig time.

---

*   *   *

(Written at Navy Radar School)

Sgt. F. V. Gardner, USMC
Pacific Fleet Schools, Box 5
Navy 91, FPO
San Francisco, California
November 11, 1944

Our Lady of Lourdes School
34508 Cedardale Road
Baltimore 15, Maryland

Dear Sister Leo:
I'm still here at Pacific Fleet Schools, but won't be for much longer. We got word yesterday from back at the base that AWS-5 is breaking up. We're going to be scattered into the 3rd Marine Air Wing. We'll stand by in Headquarters Squadron until they can find active squadrons to put us in, such as bomber, utility, photographic, transport, etc.
I'll keep you posted as to what's going on; and you keep those kids of yours on the ball.

Because our Marine divisions had been able to land on Saipan, Tinian, and Guam with complete naval and air superiority, the high command now realized there was no longer any need for our piecemeal type of air warning squadron. Marine radio and radar operators would no longer be needed to lug "Walkie Talkie" radios or portable components of electronic equipment on their backs. On the next islands we would invade, including Japan, the Army, with its heavy, permanent type installations, would handle the air warning operations. So, highly mobile, air transportable, "Marine assault" AWS-5 was to be disbanded.

Our radar operators and technicians were to be absorbed into the more stationary, permanent-type air warning squadrons. We radio operators fully expected to join aviation units that would need us as radio gunners, flying in dive bombers or torpedo planes.

(Written at hillside camp on Oahu)

November 17, 1944

Dear Mother:

As you can see from my new address, I am in a new outfit. We no sooner got back from Pacific Fleet Schools than we were put in Headquarters Squadron 3. So, in no time we're out here in the boondocks. A small bunch of us fellows, who have been together in AWS-5 for the whole time, are camped up here in the hills. We're standing by for some new developments.

*   *   *

(Written at hillside camp on Oahu)

November 20, 1944

Dear Mother:

Keynote is showing all signs of being pregnant. So, we are expecting a litter of pups in less than two months.

On November 24, 1944, the first great air attack from the Marianas against the Japanese home islands took place. One hundred B-29

Superfortresses took off from Isely Field on Saipan to bomb Tokyo. This began an almost daily schedule of bombing runs from Saipan. Later sorties were from Guam and Tinian.

The huge bombers flew a round trip of some 3000 miles north and south. Half way on their flight over the vast Central Pacific Ocean was a small island called Iwo Jima, where the Japanese had a large military air base. There was no avoiding it. The B-29s had to fly right over it and fight off the swarming fighter interceptors that rose up from the airfields below. They were able to shoot down some of our bombers before they could reach Japan. But on the return trips, they could shoot down even more, especially those airplanes that had been damaged from antiaircraft fire over Japan.

(Written at hillside camp on Oahu)

November 25, 1944

Dear Mother:

Right now I'm in Hq.3, but it won't be for long. Something new has come up. It'll be breaking in a few days. Tomorrow I'm leaving this hill site, going down to the base to join a new outfit.

The talk I was throwing around in some earlier letters about getting back to the states for a furlough was a good possibility at the time. Now it's out of the question. So, send that camera on! Hurry up or I'll be gone before it gets here.

The "base" I referred to in this letter was the Marine Corps Air Station at Ewa on the island of Oahu, Territory of Hawaii. I have no doubt that, from all the clues I had given to her in letters, my mother knew that I was on Oahu.

CHAPTER 12

*   *   *

Into Close Air Support at Ewa, Oahu

It was late 1944 on Oahu and many of the men from our squadron were sent to different locations and training sessions. Some of the men went to the northern shore of Oahu for jungle training. Others went to a tent area on a hillside overlooking the air station, for some much needed R&R. The lucky ones had a relaxing time at the Royal Hawaiian Hotel in Honolulu. I went to a Navy radar school for a few weeks with others from my squadron.

After I completed the training I joined up with my platoon mates on the hillside tent area. We were proud of how well we had performed on Saipan. We talked about how tough the battle was and what we had accomplished. We reminisced and enjoyed a couple of beers from time to time, and had no idea that our outfit was on the brink of some drastic changes. What we did not know at the time was that Marine Corps commanders were changing what we would be doing in combat and that our outfit from this point forward would have a new set of responsibilities and scope.

This new outfit, formed in the last months of 1944, was another first of its kind: Landing Force, Air Support Control Unit One (LFASCU1). Our mission changed; whereas we had been passive in reporting air enemy activity against our troops, we would now be active and in charge of our aircraft attacking the enemy positions with close air support.

Our new commanding officer was Colonel Vernon E. Megee, a Marine aviator who rose through the ranks from an enlisted man. He brought thirteen officers to the unit. These were former Navy and Marine warplane pilots, some of whom had been wounded and could not fly but they could communicate very well from the ground to our pilots in the air.

Col. Megee and his staff, under the direction of General Holland M. Smith, wanted to handle close air support and communications, not from the Naval carrier but from on the island itself. No longer would Marines be controlled by a Combat Information Center (CIC) aboard ship. Marines would command their own CIC. We would now be known as Marine Landing Force, Air Support Control Unit One, a landing force equipped with all the gear and manpower needed to dig, set up, build, manage and control a CIC of our own. We had 65 enlisted men, including 48 who had been through the battle of Saipan. The largest contingent was our group of 23 radio operators from AWS-5.

One of our more important functions was to set up and operate a Combat Information Center (CIC) ashore to match the Navy's afloat. We had to communicate with our carrier-based air squadrons in directing air strikes. We had to coordinate our efforts with artillery and naval gunfire. The CIC had to be well dug in, so we had our own bulldozer and a small construction crew.

The Central Pacific command was planning to invade two Japanese strongholds, one right after the other. Our new outfit was going to land on each of them. The most that we enlisted men could learn through scuttlebutt was that the first island would be a small one, and the second island would be much larger. In our "bull" sessions we tried to make predictions as to where the two landings might be. The first one stumped us because there were so many "small" islands to choose from. Most of us figured that the large island would be Formosa, which we know nowadays as Taiwan. As it turned out, the two islands to be invaded were places we had never heard of before. They were the closest we would land near Japan, and they had strange sounding names.

Under the parent organization, Provisional Air Support Command, our new outfit was being formed at Marine Corps Air Station, Ewa, in late November 1944. We would be ready for landing on the smaller island early in 1945. Two other units, #2 and #3, were being formed. They would join us in landing on the larger island in the spring. At the time, I didn't know where the two new units were; however, I learned many years later, from Marine Corps records, that LFASCU#3 was forming at Camp Miramar, California, and would be shipped out to the Hawaiian Islands by March 1945.

(Written at MCAS EWA, Oahu)

> *Sgt. F. V. Gardner, USMC*
> *Hq. Prov. Air Supp. Com.*
> *FMF, Pac., C/O F.P.O.*
> *San Francisco, California*
> *November 28, 1944*
>
> *Dear Mother:*
> *Well, here I am in a new outfit. The abbreviations in my return address stand for Headquarters, Provisional Air Support Command, Fleet Marine Force, Pacific.*
> *While we were up at the hill site, Saipan died of distemper. He was such a nice puppy, and growing into a fine looking dog.*
> *Tomorrow morning I'm going to fly down to one of the islands near here to get some special training.* (Maui, in the Hawaiian Islands.) *I'll be there for a few days and then fly back. I'm not going to take Keynote; will leave her with my buddies.*
> *I have to get up very early for the flight, so I'm going to hit the sack now.*

*   *   *

FRANK V. GARDNER

(Written at MCAS EWA, Oahu, T. H.)

December 4, 1944

Dear Mother:

I just returned from the other island and found your letter of November 26 waiting for me.

Your third Christmas package with the camera just arrived. Thank you. I didn't expect it so soon. As soon as I get it registered and working, I'll send you some pictures of Keynote.

I hope you enjoyed your flight to Cuba. That's your first one isn't it? I can't talk about the trip I made, but you can tell me about yours.

---

*   *   *

Missionary Sisters of Mercy
Saipan, Mariana Islands
December 12, 1944
Mrs. Marie B. Gardner
1020 19th Street, N. W.
Washington, 6 D. C.

My dear Madam:

By way of Father Dolan I received your lovely letter of October 11, which made me very happy. I had wanted to answer right away, but because of some difficulty with my vision, I was unable to write for two months. Now that I am capable, I am paying off my correspondence debts, beginning first with Francis. I wrote to him in English, although with some difficulty, but I am writing to you in Spanish so you can study it. You can answer me in English if you like.

I am very sorry for the trouble I caused you with the wrong address in my first letter. I hope you will not have any difficulty in receiving this one.

How pleased I am that your daughter is so happy as a religious. Please ask her to pray hard for us and for our mission. Our work here is that of educating the children, especially young ladies, which everywhere is difficult, but here it presents major problems.

I pray for you and your family, but, especially for Francis, who is the one most in need, without a doubt; that the Lord will preserve him and return him safely to your side; that the Divine Infant will keep all of you in his graces and blessings; and that all of you will enjoy a Merry Christmas and a Happy New Year.

Your loving servant in Christ
Sister Angelica Salaverria

*   *   *

(Written at MCAS EWA, Oahu, T. H.)

December 31, 1944

Dear Mother:

I just received your letters of December 1, 2, and 3, telling me of your flight to Cherry Point. I hope you'll be able to make another flight to Cuba later on.

It's very possible that this'll be my last letter for some time.

*   *   *

(Written at MCAS EWA, Oahu, T. H.)

January 8, 1945

Dear Sister Leo:

Yes, we're going out again; and you won't hear from me for a long time. You, more than the others, I think, understand a little better what's behind a fighting man's inability to write, etc. A war, just like your mission, takes up an awful lot of a person's time.

A little incident that happened yesterday certainly warmed all of our hearts. Keynote gave birth to eight healthy little puppies.

On January 9, 1945, General MacArthur made his second major landing in the Philippines. This time it was on Luzon, the main and largest island. Again, it was General Walter Krueger's Sixth Army that landed four infantry divisions other than those at Leyte. MacArthur, again, waded ashore from a landing craft. Ecstatic Filipinos welcomed him at the beach. A twenty-mile-long beachhead was established without much opposition, at Lingayen Gulf, 110 miles north of Manila. The Army troops advanced easily four miles inland on the first day.

On January 10, a Marine photographer came to our barracks at Ewa and took some photos of Keynote and the puppies when they were only three days old. He also took one of Keynote and me. The Marine publicity office sent the latter photo to the Washington, D. C., newspapers. Accompanying the photo was the following press release, which made a slight error as to the sex of Keynote:

> JAP DOG JOINS MARINES—Marine Sgt. Frank Gardner of 1020 19th St. N.W., Washington, D. C., is pictured with the Japoodle he rescued during the Saipan battle. In that invasion,

Gardner, a radio operator at an outpost, found a starving, shell-shocked, and bewildered pup. The Sgt. shared with him his rations and shelter, giving him the name "Keynote." Now at a Marine aviation base in the Central Pacific, "Keynote" is well fed, rapidly adapting himself to a "dog's life" in the American way. MARINE CORPS PHOTO 94610

Two Washington newspapers printed the photo of Keynote and me. One paper included a short story. In one instance, a newspaper editor mistakenly tried to improve on the Marine Corps press release, which had clearly stated, "Central Pacific." The unknowing editor, in writing the caption for the picture in his newspaper, had changed it to "South Pacific."

Many people during the war, and still today, have the erroneous impression that the Marines in World War II were always in the South Pacific. The facts are that the six Marine divisions fought eleven major battles in World War II. Of these, eight were in the Central Pacific, all north of the Equator.

Early in January of 1945, my promotion to staff sergeant came through. The first return address showing my new rating shows up on the envelope of the following letter sent to my sister, Mary, at St. Joseph's College in Emmitsburg.
(Written at MCAS, EWA, Oahu, T. H.)

January 13, 1945

Dear Mary:

The pups are coming along fine and Keynote is proving to be a very competent mother.

A photographer came over the other day to take pictures of Keynote and the pups.

Yes, I should write Gram and Uncle Lud. I have on very infrequent occasions. The difficulty lies in their not responding, which is easily understood. I'll write them within the week.

In the photo above (left to right), Donald K. Soderholm, Robert E. Thompson, William C. Herrman, and Johnnie F. Peek of LFASCU One, each hold two of Keynote's puppies at MCAS, EWA. Tom Seabourne, shown at left, of former AWS-5, holds his puppy.

(MCAS EWA)

> *January 20, 1945*
>
> **Dear Mary:**
>
> *A swabbie just walked by, selling magazines, and you should have seen Keynote jump up and bark at him. She is still not used to sailors, even after seeing them at the Navy base while I was in Radar school.*
>
> *The pups have all opened their eyes by now.*
>
> *I received your box the other day. Thank you so much for the collar.*
>
> *That was really the best thing there.* (Dog collar?)
>
> *The next time you hear of Marines storming ashore on an enemy stronghold, you'll know where I am.*
>
> *If this happens to be my last letter 'till then, let me say: "So long for a while."*

On January 25, 1945, LFASCU One boarded the *USS Thurston*, PA 77, at Pearl Harbor. My sailing log shows that we weighed anchor and vacated the harbor the same day. Our convoy was formed up off shore the next day. There, we received mail and sent our last letters home before departing the Hawaiian Islands.

(Written aboard ship, off shore from Oahu)

> *January 26, 1945*
>
> **Dear Mother:**
>
> *We boarded ship yesterday. I had a good sleep last night.*
>
> *I just got your congratulating card today. Pretty cute! All the fellows got a kick out of it.*

> *Well, I left Keynote with her pups back at the base with one of my buddies. All eight are promised out. I only hope Keynote is passed along through the right hands so that I can get her back when I return.*

*   *   *

(Written aboard ship, off shore from Oahu)

> *January 26, 1945*
>
> *Dear Sister Leo:*
> *We boarded ship yesterday, the day we've been waiting for, so impatiently, for so long. This is the longest wait we've ever had.**
> *Enclosed you'll find $10.00 you can probably use until you hear from me again.*

*   (Our scheduled invasion was delayed one month because our warships had been tied up following the Luzon landing in the Philippines. FVG 3-7-95)

*   *   *

(Written aboard ship, off shore from Oahu)

January 26, 1945

Dear Mary:

Yesterday we boarded ship. I left Keynote behind with the pups, entrusted to a buddy of mine. All the puppies will be given out in about three weeks to fellows from the former AWS-5, staying behind. I'm going to save that Valentine you sent me. Enclosed find $5.00 bill might be able to use between now and the time you hear from me again.

Below are shown profile drawings from Jane's "War at Sea 1897-1997 Centennial Edition (London 1997). They depict six Navy and Marine Corps aircraft used for close air support in the Pacific.

The first "F" indicates fighter plane. The number "4" or "6" stands for the model number. The second "F" stands for the manufacturer, Grumman. "M" is for General Motors, which made the later models. "U" stands for Vought-Sikorsky, or Chance Vought.

F4F Fighter/bomber

F6F Fighter/bomber (Photo of F6F in flight on Page 104.)

F4U Fighter/bomber (Photo of F4U in flight on Page 158.)

"SB" is for scout/bomber. "D" is for the manufacturer, Douglas; "C" for Curtiss. "TB" is for torpedo bomber. Grumman made the earlier TBF. The Eastern Aircraft Division of General Motors, made later models of the torpedo bomber with the designation, "M."

SBD Scout/bomber or dive bomber (Photo of SBD in flight on Page 50.)

SB2C Scout/bomber or dive bomber

TBF or TBM Torpedo bomber (Lt. George H. W. Bush piloted *Avenger*: P. 127.)

Shown here on liberty in Honolulu, Hawaii, from left to right:
Herman Mastrogiovanni, John Cangelosi, and Al Buff

CHAPTER 13

*   *   *

Iwo Jima

On January 27, 1945, we in LFASCU #1 departed the Hawaiian Islands aboard the *USS Thurston*. As in the previous year, our convoy of ships headed southwest toward the Marshall Islands. Again, we learned of our objective once we were in the open seas. The small island we were to invade was Iwo Jima in the Bonin Islands. The Japanese referred to the Bonins as the Nanpo Shoto, meaning Volcano Islands. The planners at Makalapa had labeled this invasion Operation Detachment, a name long since forgotten.

One of our ships carried Fleet Admiral Chester W. Nimitz and his staff. The Commander in Chief, Pacific Fleet (CINCPAC), would be moving his headquarters some 3,000 miles westward: from Makalapa at Pearl Harbor, across the Central Pacific, to the island of Guam in the Marianas.

We learned that Iwo Jima had a surface of only eight square miles; that its land was formed from an extinct volcano; and that it was halfway between Saipan and Tokyo, Japan. We were invading that island to capture its three airfields and to use them in our air war against Japan. In the Nanpo Shoto there were several other tips of land protruding from the ocean; but Iwo Jima, meaning Sulfur Island, was the only one of any significance on which we would land.

The Joint Chiefs of Staff had ordered the capture of Iwo Jima some six months earlier. Its capture would deny the enemy's use of those airfields against us, and, in our hands, would provide bases from which we could launch fighter escorts for our long-range bombers over Japan. One side benefit, which proved to be most significant as the war continued, was that our B-29s would have a halfway station where they could land in emergencies.

The island was five miles long and two and one-half miles wide at its widest point. The civilian population, numbering about 1,000 persons, had been evacuated from the island several months earlier. Enemy records were found after the battle, fixing the size of the garrison at around 23,000 defenders. They had constructed over seven hundred gun emplacements and pillboxes with reinforced concrete. They also dug hundreds of underground bunkers with miles of connecting tunnels. It was the most heavily fortified island invaded in the entire Pacific War.

Department of Defense Photo (USMC) 132.01
LtGen Tadimichi Kuribayashi, Imperial Japanese Army

The commanding officer of the Japanese garrison on Iwo Jima was Lieutenant General Tadimichi Kuribayashi. He had been hand picked by Emperor Hirohito for this most important assignment.

In 1928, Kuribayashi had been a thirty-seven-year old captain and deputy military attaché at the Japanese embassy in Washington. For the next two years he had crisscrossed the United States in almost constant travel, taking time to observe Americans and practice his fluent English in such diverse locales as Buffalo, New York, and the U. S. Army Cavalry School at Fort Bliss, Texas, where he studied horse-mounted combat.

Captain Kuribayashi was devoted to his family, and unhappy that Japanese policy kept his wife Toshii and young son Taro from being with him in the United States. Twice a week he wrote chatty letters home, often embellished with excellent sketches of places he had seen and people he had met. In one letter, more serious than usual during the late 1920s, he wrote:

The United States is the last country in the world Japan should fight. Its industrial potential is huge and fabulous, and the people are energetic and versatile. One must never underestimate the Americans' fighting ability.

By January 1945, on Iwo Jima, General Kuribayashi had done all he could to fortify the island and to prepare his troops for the inevitable battle. He exhorted them:

Every man will resist until the end, making his position his tomb. Every man will do his best to kill ten enemy soldiers.

The general knew that his fate was sealed but was determined to make the Americans pay dearly. The last letter he was able to send from his island fortress included a note to his children:

". . . from now on you must reconcile yourselves to living without a father."

The task of capturing Iwo Jima had been assigned to the Fifth Amphibious Corps, commanded by Major General Harry Schmidt. He had commanded the Fourth Marine Division the year before on Roi-Namur, Saipan and Tinian. Now, as Corps commander, he would have his old division plus two other Marine divisions for the invasion of Iwo Jima.

For Iwo Jima's D-Day, the Fourth and Fifth Marine Divisions were to land side by side on a two-mile stretch of beach along the narrow southeast coast of the island. The Third Marine Division would be held offshore in floating reserve until the beachhead could be expanded.

Lieutenant General Holland M. Smith had commanded the Fifth Amphibious Corps across the Central Pacific, from the atolls of the Gilbert and Marshall Islands to Saipan and Tinian in the Marianas. He was now to be commander of all expeditionary forces in the new Operation Detachment at Iwo Jima.

On February 4, our convoy dropped anchor at Eniwetok, as was done the year before, and refueled. After three days, we continued westward. On February 11, we dropped anchor off Saipan. For a few days we went through landing maneuvers off the nearby island of Tinian. On February 16, we weighed anchor and headed north toward our destination. Meanwhile, some 700 miles ahead of us, the scheduled heavy bombardment of the island began on D-Day Minus 3.

Some three months earlier, on November 11, 1944, Armistice Day, ironically, one of the earliest of our several naval bombardments had taken place at Iwo Jima, with a task force, featuring the cruisers, *Chester, Pensacola,* and *Salt Lake City.* On December 23, 1,000 additional Japanese soldiers had been landed on Iwo to reinforce the garrison there. The following day, Christmas Eve, another U. S. Navy task force, including the same three cruisers from November, bombarded the island. They sunk the two enemy transports that had brought in the new troops. Beginning on December 8, 1944, until D-Day Minus 1, there would be 73 consecutive days of high altitude bombing of Iwo Jima by B-24 Liberators from the Marianas.

Again, as at Saipan the year before, we were to have three days of concentrated, pre-invasion shelling by our largest warships. This time, instead of just three battleships, there would be six. All of these dreadnoughts were labeled, "old ladies" by their commander in charge of naval support, Rear Admiral William H. P. Blandy. They were designated OBB, old battleships.

The *Tennessee* and the *Nevada* (photos below), both salvaged from the sludge of Pearl Harbor, would bombard the landing beaches in the southeast corner. Three of the other old battleships, *Idaho, Texas,* and *Arkansas (below),* would strike coastal areas at the southern tip, including Mount Suribachi. The high ground in the center was assigned to the battleship *New York,* and the cruiser *Salt Lake City* (both, next page). Targets in the remaining northern part of the island were divided among the four other cruisers: *Chester, Pensacola, Tuscaloosa* (next page), and *Vicksburg.* There would also be ten aircraft carriers for air strikes against the island.

U.S.S. Tennessee

U.S.S. Nevada

U.S.S. Arkansas

U.S.S. New York

Every known major target on the island was numbered, then listed on a master index aboard Admiral Blandy's flagship. There were more than seven hundred targets to be hit, including blockhouses, gun emplacements, and pillboxes. Each battleship and cruiser had its own spotter plane, which it launched by catapult, which is a huge mechanical slingshot. The pilots were to send radio directions back to their ships for effective gunfire, and then give reports on hits that were made. When a target became demolished, it was to be checked off the master chart. After flying over target areas, the spotter planes, which had float pontoons instead of landing wheels, came down on the water alongside their ships and were hoisted aboard.

U.S.S. Salt Lake City

U.S.S. Tuscaloosa

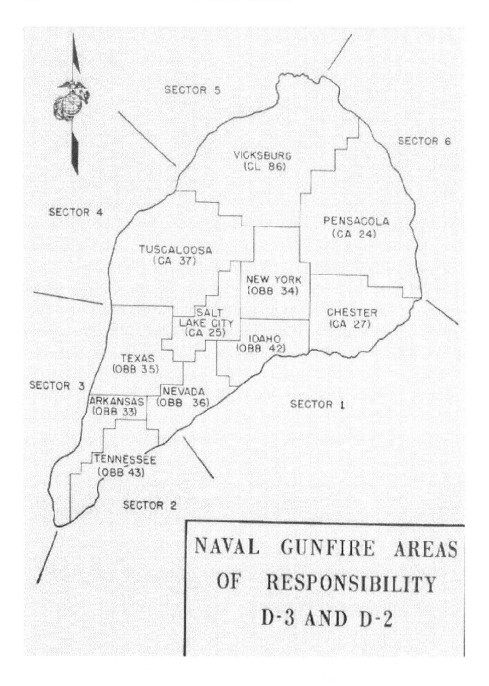

SECTOR 5

VICKSBURG
(CL 86)

SECTOR 6

SECTOR 4

PENSACOLA
(CA 24)

TUSCALOOSA
(CA 37)

NEW YORK
(OBB 34)

SALT
LAKE CITY
(CA 25)

CHESTER
(CA 27)

IDAHO
(OBB 42)

TEXAS
(OBB 35)

SECTOR 3

NEVADA
(OBB 36)

ARKANSAS
(OBB 33)

SECTOR 1

TENNESSEE
(OBB 43)

SECTOR 2

NAVAL GUNFIRE AREAS
OF RESPONSIBILITY
D-3 AND D-2

The weather turned bad very early the first morning of naval bombardment, bringing heavy rain and zero visibility. During the remainder of the day, there were only a few opportunities for the aerial spotters to relay radio directions for naval gunfire. When evening came and the fleet pulled back from the island, aerial photographs showed that only seventeen targets had been destroyed out of about seven hundred. Over the next two days, only sixteen more blockhouses and seventeen additional coastal guns had been put out of action.

Meanwhile, on D-Day Minus 2, well before our troop convoy arrived on the scene, 102 Navy and Marine expert swimmers from Underwater Demolition Teams (UDTs) went into action. Poised aboard small rubber boats that were lashed alongside twelve rocket-firing gunboats, these swimmers or "frogmen" were attired only in swim trunks, face masks, tennis shoes, and flippers. To guard against the wintertime cold water, they were coated with camouflage grease or cocoa butter. The UDT swimmers were largely volunteers, who performed their specialty in several major amphibious assaults in the Pacific. Following the war, the Marine volunteers were phased out, and it became strictly a Navy operation. Today, we know them as Navy Seals.

With rockets firing, the gunboats made a run toward the beach and dropped off the swimmers 250 yards off shore. The frogmen swam about 100 yards apart from each other. They stayed underwater as much as possible, coming up only for air. This was to avoid possible enemy rifle and machine-gun fire from the cliffs and high ground. (Scuba-type oxygen tanks had not yet been developed.) The swimmers found no serious obstacles underwater or at the beaches. Then, still under covering rocket fire, they swam back to be picked up offshore.

Meanwhile, all twelve gunboats were hit by heavy artillery fire from the island. Nine of the boats were put out of commission. So, retrieving the frogmen turned into a general melee, with other ships having to come in close to assist. However, only one of the frogmen was reported missing at the end of the day. The only other casualty among swimmers was a cut that one of them received from an underwater rock.

The cruiser *Pensacola,* which was blasting Mount Suribachi from about 250 yards off shore, took six heavy artillery hits within three minutes. The ship's Combat Information Center was knocked out; the executive officer and sixteen men were killed. Exploding ammunition wounded 127 sailors. The *Tennessee* went in close to lay down smoke for hiding the stricken gunboats. It took a minor hit, wounding six men. Also hit was the destroyer, *Leutze*, which also was laying down smoke and fishing survivors from the sea. Seven men were killed and thirty-three wounded, including the skipper, Commander B. Robbins.

The fleet that gathered around Iwo Jima on the morning of D-Day, February 19, 1945, including warships and transport vessels, numbered 800 ships. This was now the largest cross-ocean fleet on record in the Central Pacific Area, exceeding by twenty-five the size of the fleet involved at Saipan the year before. The number of capital ships had increased in a few days more than six-fold. The naval support armada now had eight battleships, nineteen cruisers, and forty-four destroyers. The bombardment began at 6:40 in the morning and continued without let up for one hour and twenty minutes.

At H-Hour minus sixty minutes, 8 o'clock in the morning, it was time for the air strikes by carrier-based aircraft. Seventy-two Navy planes were first to crisscross the landing beaches and the terraces inland with bombing and strafing runs. These included Grumman-made F6F *Hellcat* fighters and Douglas-made SBD *Dauntless* dive-bombers. The Navy pilots then headed back to their carriers to refuel and rearm.

Next, an all-Marine squadron of forty-eight gull-wing fighter/bombers from a large, fast carrier came in. In briefing the flying leathernecks prior to the strike, our commanding officer of LFASCU #1, Colonel Vernon E. Megee, himself a Marine aviator, had encouraged them: "Go in and drag your bellies on the beach." They were flying F4U *Corsairs*, made by Vought-Sikorsky, with a top speed over 400 miles per hour. These fastest fighter planes in the fleet unleashed their "whistling death"  bombing and strafing runs on Mt. Suribachi and the two-mile-long landing beach on the eastern side of the island.

Those air strikes, which continued for thirty minutes, were conducted under the command of our C.O., Col. Vernon E. Megee. He was using a Navy Combat Information Center aboard one of the aircraft carriers of Task Force 58. That Navy CIC would continue coordinating his air strikes until our outfit, Landing Force, Air Support Control Unit #1, could get ashore and set up land operations.

At H-Hour minus thirty minutes, the first wave of amphibious tractors crossed the "line of departure" for the thirty-minute run to the landing beaches. These first landing craft, called Amtracs,

H-hour at Iwo Jima, 19 February 1945.
Department of Defense Photo (USMC) NH62811.

carried no landing troops, but their machine guns were blazing as they hit the beach at 9:02 A.M. By this time, naval gunfire had been lifted 400 yards inland. Then six waves of Amtracs followed, carrying Marine riflemen. A rolling naval barrage would continue inland as more Marines came ashore and moved forward. Each Amtrac wave landed five minutes apart, disgorging 1,360 men. The Amtracs were followed by hundreds of Higgins boats, or LCVPs, carrying thousands more men from the Fourth and Fifth Marine Divisions to expand the narrow beachhead.

The Japanese allowed the first waves of Marines to clog the beaches. On the steep terraces beyond the beach, the struggling leathernecks became mired in the loose, black volcanic ash. Then the enemy artillery, from the heights of Suribachi to the south and the high ground to the north, opened up with a vengeance on the invaders. The assaulting Marines suffered heavy casualties from the outset; but they kept moving and pushed on below Mount Suribachi, across the narrow neck of land to the western beach. By nightfall, 566 had been killed and 1,854 wounded by the enemy's merciless artillery and machine-gun fire. Total Marines casualties on D-Day: 2,420.

Unlike Saipan, however, where hospital ships had arrived three days after D-Day, the *Solace* and *Samaritan* were on station at Iwo from the beginning of the campaign. Each was equipped with every life saving tool available to stateside hospitals. The medical staff on each ship averaged twenty physicians, forty nurses, and two-hundred corpsmen. The auxiliary hospital ship *Pinkney*, an attack transport converted solely for medical duty, was nearby with four "Landing Ships, Tank," (LSTs) equipped for surgery.

Because of this tremendous medical support from D-Day forward, my outfit, waiting to debark, did not see wounded men being brought back from the beach to our troop transport as we had at Saipan. Most of the wounded were taken straight to the hospital ships lying off Iwo Jima.

However, there were still a few troopships that had to take wounded aboard when the hospital ships filled up. Ralph Lee Edwards, of Stafford, Virginia, gives an account of such activity in a book, entitled, "A Virginia Marine on Iwo Jima." Ralph, a member of the 30th Replacement Draft, was in a large pool of Marines aboard the *Bayfield*. They would not be committed to battle for at least a few days, until the Fourth Marine Division would have a chance to assess its casualty losses and issue a call for replacements.

Apparently, Ralph and the replacement Marines spent most of the first two days unloading food, supplies, and ammunition from the ship to go ashore. He recalls that as the hospital ships filled up, the *Bayfield* began taking the wounded aboard. His contingent of replacements went ashore on February 23 to take their places on the front line with the 24th Marines.

One of the gallant warriors who died on Iwo Jima's beach on D-Day was Marine Gunnery Sergeant John Basilone of Raritan, New Jersey.

Already a Marine Corps legend, he was the first leatherneck to be awarded the Medal of Honor in World War II.

Back in 1942, on a black October night in the steaming jungles of Guadalcanal, Basilone had single-handedly wiped out a company of Japanese trying to overrun his position on the Tenaru River. He fired a machine gun and his Colt .45 pistol through the night to stem the onslaught. When his gun was knocked out, he took another from a fallen Marine and had to cradle it in his arms to keep firing. He managed to stop a screaming banzai attack and held out alone until dawn brought reinforcements. Nearly one hundred enemy dead were sprawled around his cut-off outpost.

After he recovered from the burns his hands and arms sustained from holding the searing-hot machine gun barrel, he became a celebrity back home, making public appearances. He could have remained stateside, training troops and selling war bonds; but he longed to get back with the Marines who were fighting the war. He requested another combat assignment, and saying farewell to his new wife, also a Marine, joined the new Fifth Marine Division, being formed in 1944.

Now, on the beach at Iwo Jima, with the invasion just ninety minutes old, Basilone was urging a team of gunners to haul their guns off the beach, when a Japanese mortar blast killed him instantly. His body lay in the black, volcanic ash with his left arm stretched forward showing a tattoo: "Death before Dishonor."

At Iwo Jima it took our unit longer to get ashore than the D-Plus-1 of Saipan. This beachhead area was so restricted that it was not until D-Plus-3 that we could land and find a suitable place to construct our Combat Information Center. It took a couple of days for us to get everything set up in a fairly safe location.

First, PFC Francesco G. Merle, our bulldozer operator, had to excavate a large cavity in the loose volcanic ash. Then we all pitched in to load and place sandbags to make a foundation of high walls. A crew under direction of Technical Sergeant George Konchar, our carpenter, then went to work with a supply of lumber to construct the benches, tables, and work areas of the Combat Information Center. Meanwhile, we "turned to" in helping Master Technical Sergeant Willard K. Webster, our communications chief, set up radio equipment and communication lines. On D-Plus-5 our Combat Information Center went into operation and we took over air-support control from the shipboard CIC off shore.

We camped in an area between Mount Suribachi and Motoyama Airfield #1 on a slope angling down toward the western beach. We dug deep, two-man foxholes where we slept each night. To ward off the rain, we stretched our pup tent across the top opening, and anchored it around the edges with sandbags.

Frank Gardner shown here in his foxhole.

General Holland Smith said all of us on Iwo were at the front lines. Even we in the rear were constantly in danger of being hit by Japanese artillery or rockets. We called the rockets, "Screaming Meamies," from the high-pitched sound they made as they streaked overhead every night for the first two weeks. They always seemed to land up against Mount Suribachi or out in the water. They were between two and three feet long and were about nine inches in diameter.

Meanwhile, on D-Day Plus 1, the Fourth Division's 23rd Marines had captured most of Chidori Airfield or Motoyama #1. That regiment held the center of the line. The Fourth Division's 25th Marines were on the east side, and the Fifth Division's 27th Marines were on the west.

The Fifth Division's 28th Regiment was attacking an enemy force cut off at Mount Suribachi to the south. Finally, after four days of bitter fighting, the 28th Marines captured the 556-foot extinct volcano and planted a small American flag on its summit on the morning of D-Day Plus 4, February 23, 1945.

General Holland M. Smith and Secretary of the Navy James Forrestal were on Iwo Jima's Green Beach that morning, watching the action on Mt. Suribachi. Secretary Forrestal turned to General Smith and said, "Holland, this means a Marine Corps for another five hundred years."

Because the original flag was too small to be appreciated, a much larger one was sent up the mountain later in the day for all Marines on the island to see. Associated Press Photographer Joseph Rosenthal happened to be on the scene when five Marines and a Navy medical corpsman raised the second flag. The famous photograph he snapped at that moment has become a Marine Corps symbol. (See below.) Three of the men who raised that flag never left the island; they were killed in action before the five-week battle had ended.

The four Marines closest to the camera are, from left to right, Ira Hayes, Franklin Sousley, John Bradley (Navy medical corpsman), and Harlon Block. Obscured on the other side are Michael Strank and Rene Gagnon. The three who were killed in action later on the island were Mike Strank and Harlon Block, both on March 1; Franklin Sousley on March 21.

On D-Day Plus 4, the news of Mt. Suribachi's capture spread through all the troops elsewhere on the island. There were cheers from units that were not preoccupied with the enemy at the time.

When I heard the news, I was busy with our communications work in the CIC, so I couldn't celebrate too much. However, later in the day, I went outside and peered up to see that American flag flying atop Mount Suribachi. I had a deep sense of pride and relief for what had been accomplished.

With the extinct volcano now in our hands, we no longer feared the enemy firing down on us from behind. Their artillery, from the northern high ground, was still shelling us; but it was random firing, no longer being directed by their radio spotters on Mount Suribachi.

Now with the mountain captured, it was thought that the western beach, very close to our camp, might be put into operation for unloading supplies. One day one of our cargo ships, loaded with explosives, approached the western beach. It anchored just a couple of hundred yards offshore. Obviously, its captain was not aware that enemy artillery north of Motoyama Airfield #2 was still within range to fire on it. Before the ship could begin unloading its explosive cargo, Japanese artillery spotted it and began firing. I, along with some others from LFASCU One, watched from our camp with fascination as enemy artillery shells started splashing in the water, without exploding, nearby the big ship. Other interested observers, we learned, were watching also from Fifth Amphibious Corps headquarters just up the slope next to our unit. They were Lt. General Holland M. Smith, and Major General Harry Schmidt.

One shell fell close enough to wound a sailor on the stern. The next salvo fell ahead of the ship. Now, the enemy gunners needed only to adjust their aim to hit the target; however, fortunately for all of us, the ship picked up speed and departed quickly enough to get out of artillery range.

Since D-Day on Iwo Jima, there had been four days of uninterrupted fighting by the two Marine divisions driving north from Mount Suribachi. So, the Third Marine Division's 21st Regiment was called in from floating reserve to relieve the exhausted 23rd Marines, who had

A soldier (judging from pockets) is receiving communion, surrounded by Marines.

just captured most of the first airfield. The regiments on either side, which also had stormed the beaches, were relieved about the same time. The 25th

Marines were relieved by the Fourth Division's 24th, and the 27th Marines by the Fifth Division's 26th.

The pattern for relieving regiments on the front line was, as follows. After three or four days, the division's regiment in the rear would relieve one of the two on the front line. Each infantry regiment would follow a similar pattern with its three battalions at the line.

On the afternoon of D-Plus-5, the Third Marine Division, minus its 3rd Regiment (3rd Marines), was committed to the battle. It came ashore to take its place in the center for the drive north, with its 9th Marine Regiment joining the 21st, already on the front line. All of its non-infantry support battalions also came ashore. So, the Third Division would operate with only two of its infantry regiments.

In committing the Third Marine Division with one regiment short, General Howlin Mad Smith felt it could operate well enough in the center, having two full Marine divisions on either side. The 3rd Marines were sent back to Guam to preserve at least one intact Marine regiment for spearheading the amphibious invasion of Japan scheduled later in 1945. Meanwhile, the 28th Marines spent about a week mopping up on Mount

Suribachi before moving into the front line facing north. By the end of the first week, each division had a field hospital in operation at a fairly safe location in the rear areas.

For air-support control, we in LFASCU One were also bivouacked in a fairly safe location. We maintained radio communication with our carrier planes; also with forward observers for artillery and naval-gunfire on the ground. This way we could choose the enemy targets that needed to be hit from the air. We had experienced pilots with us on the ground. They kept in radio contact with the airborne pilot called our air coordinator. He knew the terrain features and target locations. After an assignment of two or three hours on station, one carrier-based air coordinator would pass on his duties to another.

When a new squadron reported on station for air strikes, the air coordinator would briefly explain the mission to all flyers and lead them on a "dummy run" over the target area. When they all acknowledged that they had seen their targets, he would send them on a "live run." Very often, our planes were able to hit targets that were largely inaccessible to the limited trajectory of artillery and naval gunfire because the enemy positions were concealed in canyons or on reverse sides of ridges or cliffs.

On February 26, D-Plus-7, the first of the Army's P-51 Mustang fighter planes were able to land on Motoyama #1. These sleek, speedy aircraft were the first contingent of some 300 that were to provide fighter escort for B-29 Superfortress bombers from the Marianas that would fly over Iwo on their way to bombing missions in Japan.

Around this time, Admiral Raymond Spruance ordered his large, fast carriers north, away from Iwo Jima, for a series of strikes around Tokyo. This removed eight Marine air squadrons of the vaunted F4U *Corsair* fighters from our close air support operations on Iwo. The remaining, mostly Navy squadrons, from the smaller escort carriers, tried to pick up the slack. However, they were limited in their capabilities, lacking the expertise of our Marine fliers who specialized in supporting their leatherneck comrades on the ground.

As an alternative, our commander, Colonel Megee, enlisted the aid of the newly arrived P-51 squadron, whose Army pilots, although they could not perform dive-bombing missions, were good at glide bombing, and they were enthusiastic. He instructed them to arm their regular 1000-pound bombs with 12-second fuses; then directed them against the cliffs and bluffs along the flanks of the attacking Marines, with spectacular success in blasting enemy caves.

Meanwhile, we radio operators performed various jobs for the air-support mission. Along with the basic job of maintaining radio contact with our fliers, we had to see that all air-to-ground radio transmissions, and some air-to-air, were recorded properly. For this, we took our turns in the CIC, listening with earphones, and typing verbatim the conversations we heard on manual typewriters. Usually, this involved a dialogue between the air coordinator and the squadron leader, although, at times we had to "copy" the remarks or acknowledgments of the squadron's individual pilots. They always identified themselves by airplane number.

We also took our turns on night watch in the CIC. On these occasions, I was appalled to see the official casualty figures of our Marine fighting units that were reported each day to the Fifth Amphibious Corps. After the first three or four days, when our casualties of more than 5,000 were reported in the newspapers back home, President Roosevelt did not want the American people to become alarmed. So, the White House gave orders that no further mention of American losses would be made in official communiqués from Iwo Jima.

Our daily casualty figures were mounting faster than during any previous battle of the Pacific War. The fanatical resistance of the island's defenders was most impressive. This was fueled to some extent by an official proclamation General Kuribayashi had issued well before D-Day. Marines found copies of it in the first destroyed bunkers on the beaches. As the battle continued, our troops found more copies in caves, tunnels, pillboxes, inland bunkers, and on the bodies of enemy dead. In classic, bold Japanese characters, the proclamation read:

The Iwo Jima Courageous Battle Vows

Above all else, we shall dedicate ourselves to the defense of this island, with our entire strength.

We shall grasp bombs, charge the enemy tanks, and destroy them.

We shall infiltrate into the midst of the enemy and annihilate them.

With every salvo we will, without fail, kill the enemy

Each man will make it his duty to kill ten of the enemy before dying.

**Until we are destroyed to the last man, we shall harass
the enemy by guerrilla tactics.**

By end of the first week on Iwo Jima, our casualties had passed
the 9,000 mark, but that figure was not announced to the press corps.
The Japanese casualties were probably about the same number, most
of them dead. However, there was no way that all of these could be
counted during the fighting because so many were entombed in sealed
caves, tunnels, and bunkers. The enemy totals, therefore, would have
to wait until the end of the campaign. Then we could examine enemy
personnel records for an insight into the size of their garrison. At
times, later in the campaign, there were so many dead bodies on both
sides strewn on the battlefield that burial details could not keep up
with the volume.

Although the nights were still fairly cool, most of the days were clear
and sunny, so the temperatures would rise considerably, bloating the dead
bodies, which emitted the sickening stench of death over the battlefield.
This, of course, generated swarms of flies in the affected areas. As the
bodies of dead Marines accumulated at our three division cemeteries
awaiting burial, they were sprayed routinely with disinfectant by hand-held
equipment. (See below.)

When too many Japanese
bodies piled up in forward areas,
low flying, light aircraft sprayed
disinfectant over no man's land
from above. There were many
instances when enemy soldiers
would sneak out at night to
recover some of their bodies and hide them in caves. As our advanced
units moved forward, the remaining enemy bodies were collected and
buried in mass graves.

By March 1, the Third Marine Division had captured all of
Motoyama #2 and was approaching the smallest of Iwo's three
airfields, the unfinished Motoyama #3. From that high position,

Japanese artillery was still able to lay down harassing fire on the Seabees, working feverishly to make Motoyama #1 ready for B-29 landings.

On March 4, a Superfortress heavy bomber named *"Dinah Might,"* damaged over Japan, made an emergency landing on Iwo Jima. Its crewmen jumped out of the Army B-29 and kissed the ground in a gesture of gratitude for their safe landing.

"Dinah Might," the first crippled B-29 to make an emergency landing on Iwo Jima during the fighting, is surrounded by Marines and Seabees on 4 March 1945.

A day or two later, LFASCU One received a radio distress call after completing air strikes for the day. Another B-29 was flying south over the Central Pacific Ocean, and was short on fuel because of damage from enemy antiaircraft fire over Japan. It would not be able to reach home base 700 miles away. The airplane, with its ten-man crew, would have to splash down in the ocean unless it could make an emergency landing on Iwo Jima.

We informed the pilot that he could attempt an emergency landing on Motoyama #1. He should first circle off shore to use up fuel for making the landing attempt less hazardous. He should remain south of the island, out of the enemy sight. Also, by coming in later, under cover of darkness, he would be less likely to draw artillery fire from the enemy-held high ground.

At nightfall, with the airfield in complete darkness and the aircraft flying without lights, it approached the island. One of our landlubber pilots, who was monitoring the flight on a radar screen, directed the bomber pilot by radio to drop down low to 100 feet of altitude, with Mount Suribachi on his left as he lined up with the north-south runway. Another of our land-based pilots at the airfield, "radio talked" the aircraft to a near perfect touchdown on the mile-long runway. Because of the darkness, the B-29 pilot didn't use all the available landing space on the runway. Therefore, his wheel brakes were not sufficient to prevent the big plane from rolling into an embankment at the far end of the airstrip. The impact with the mound of black volcanic ash bent one of its propellers.

The next morning a few of us from air support went over to the airfield, where I snapped a photo of the B-29 up against the mound of black ash with its bent propeller. Later that day with its damage repaired, the huge bomber was able to continue its return flight back to the Marianas.

I snapped another photo at the airfield. It was of Radio Operator Al Buff, wearing his favorite baseball peak cap, leaning up against an Army night-fighter airplane, called the Black Widow. He wanted  to leave the impression that he was the pilot. The nose of the aircraft sported the painting of a scantily clad woman with the caption, "BAT OUT A HELL"

The battle continued in the northern part of the island through the middle of March. Our advances in that rocky, cavernous terrain were measured day by day, yard by yard. The Japanese soldiers were extremely well disciplined, holding their concealment, firing on us as we advanced. On rare occasions we had to engage in hand-to-hand combat. We sealed their cave openings with flame-throwers and explosives. Our warplanes dropped napalm ahead of us to burn out heavily defended canyons before we advanced.

As the battle progressed, crippled B-29s began landing daily for repairs or refueling. In all, until the war ended some five months later, the two larger airfields on Iwo Jima had accepted 2,251 emergency or unscheduled landings of B-29s returning to their home bases on Saipan, Tinian, and Guam. The standard crew numbered eleven men, although the huge four-motor airplanes were known to fly at times with only ten. A simple calculation of the 2,200 landings multiplied by ten crewmen would indicate that 22,000 persons found refuge on Iwo Jima.

We know that many of the Superfortresses had to land on Iwo more than once, including *Dinah Might,* which landed there three times although with some different crewmen. Even if one third of the landings had been repeats or marginal, that would leave some 14,000 Army air crewmen who would have gone down at sea had it not been for the airfields on Iwo Jima. The island where 6,000 Marines sacrificed their lives became a refuge for those airmen in that vast Pacific Ocean.

The first letter I sent home from Iwo Jima was a hand-written, one-page V-Mail note in a postage-free envelope, dated March 3, 1945. I used the Fleet Post Office return address, as required. However, I was able to let mother know where I was because the censors had announced to the troops on the island that we could divulge our location in letters sent back home. The U. S. Postal Service imprinted the postmark, dated March 10, 1945. This would suggest that the letter had been routed through either Hawaii or San Francisco. Therefore, I would gather that mother probably received the March 3, free-postage V-Mail somewhat later than the longer letter I sent home with a six-cent airmail stamp on March 5.

March 3, 1945

Dear Mother:

Iwo Jima is about the dirtiest island in the Pacific, and one of the smallest. (Big troubles come in small packages.)

I'm fine and healthy. Hope to get off here soon.

I received a few letters while aboard ship, but will have to answer them later.

The envelope of the second letter shows the postmark of the U. S. Navy, dated March 5, 1945. This indicates that it was processed by one of the Navy ships off shore the same day I wrote it. So, it probably reached mother earlier, especially since the envelope bears a six-cent airmail stamp. I typed the second letter in our CIC at 5:47 in the morning while on night watch.

Iwo Island
0547
March 5, 1945

Dear Mother:

I'll have to wait until I get off here to answer those letters. I haven't written Mary or Dorothy from here, but I trust you'll give them the word. Things aren't going so badly now. All the major fighting should be over in a couple of days.

This is a treeless, sulfuric, black-sand hellhole of 8 square miles, with a big volcano and three airfields. We never did care too much for the volcano; our prime interest is in the airfields.

The Navy is doing a wonderful job.

I think about home an awful lot. I think about all I hope to do when all this is over. I think about the girl I will marry and the home I will make.

On board ship coming over, we were fortunate enough to have a Catholic chaplain with us. He said mass for us every day and held services for the other faiths on Sunday and Saturday.

There is hardly any vegetation at all on the island. We haven't had too much rain. During the days our vehicles raise constant clouds of black dust, which settles everywhere. We call it island pepper and involuntarily season our chow with it. I've been down to the beach a few times to bathe with salt-water soap. Did you ever see a black beach? Well, take any beach back home and spread coal dust all over it and you'll get what I mean.

One pest we are fortunate not to be bothered with is the mosquito. The flies here are not half as bad as they were on Saipan. A likely reason is that the weather here is cooler and we have a good wind most of the time.

I'll have to sign off now. I'm going off watch.

There's a lot more I could write, but at present I'm at a loss for words and time.

I'll write a good long letter when I embark again.

The beach where we bathed with salt-water soap was on the western side of the island, not cluttered and clogged like the landing beach on the eastern side.

During our struggle for Iwo Jima, we were not expecting to find any civilians, since they, supposedly, had all been evacuated the year before. Yet, one day in the third week of battle, two Asian women surrendered to our front line troop on the battlefield. They turned out to be what the Japanese called "comfort women." They were quickly whisked away to be debriefed by our intelligence officers on Iwo. Within the next day or two, they should have been flown down to Guam for extensive interviews at Pacific Fleet headquarters.

Forty-nine years later, on November 24, 1994, the Japanese government considered sending personal letters of apology to those women who were still alive. The 1994 plan provided for providing monetary compensation to the women from a private fund made up of voluntary contributions from the Japanese public. A Reuters report from Tokyo in the Washington Times of November 25, 1994, stated the following: Some 200,000 women, mostly Asian, acted as sex slaves for Japanese soldiers in the Pacific and Far East during the war.

During the war, U. S. Marines landed on at least 100 different islands. Three in the South Pacific were fairly large. Most of the others, in the Central Pacific, were much smaller. On some of the atolls or islets, only a battalion or smaller unit may have landed.

The six Marine divisions were involved in eleven major island battles, where 88 Medals of Honor were earned. Marines on Iwo Jima earned 22 Medals of Honor. This was one fourth of the total such medals earned by Marines during the war.

Also, four medical corpsmen received Medals of Honor on Iwo Jima. Because of inter-service distinctions, however, they were listed separately from the 22 Marines cited above. Despite those distinctions, however, when Navy corpsmen served with us, we considered them Marines.

For example, in our small unit one Navy corpsman was assigned to care for our immediate medical needs and injuries in the field. He stayed with us all through the war. He was John F. Church, Pharmacist's Mate, First Class. He wore our uniform, our insignia. He marched with us, trained with us, he was one of us. He endured the same hardships. He was our corpsman. We all considered him to be a Marine.

Many years later I learned the full accounts of those Marines who received the Congressional Medal of Honor for their actions on Iwo Jima. Here I shall recite the story of just one of them, Joseph Julian. His action above and beyond the call of duty occurred when the battle for Iwo Jima was in its third week, on March 9, 1945. I found the following written account in Bill D. Ross's book, "IWO JIMA: Legacy of Valor."

Heavy and costly fighting still faced the Marines across the island on D-Day plus eighteen, especially in the convoluted terrain of the Fifth Division sector. So formidable were the natural defenses, so deadly and determined was enemy resistance in the zone, that less than fifty yards were gained during the next forty-eight hours.

Major obstacle was a long and low ridge, jutting southeast from Kitano Point, a heavily fortified escarpment overlooking a deep draw manned by suicidal troops. It would take fifteen days to finally wipe out what would become the final pocket of organized Japanese resistance on Iwo.

Two battalions from the 27th Regiment—Justin Duryea's First and John Antonelli's Second—both moved into the death-dealing maze shortly after daybreak. Both commanders were out of the battle by early afternoon, maimed by a land mine as, together, they were working their way to the front to see if anything could be done to spring the advance.

One of Duryea's men, Platoon Sergeant Joseph Julian, was doing everything imaginable to quell the firestorm of small arms and mortar fire from the ridge . . .

Julian was a twenty-six-year-old career Marine from historic Sturbridge Village in Massachusetts. Since D-Day he had defied the odds in countless rampages that reminded his platoon of the devil-be-damned attitude of his gung-ho friend, PFC Jacklyn Lucas. Now, with the attack less than fifteen minutes old, Julian's platoon was pinned down by machine gun fire from several caves.

Crawling forward some fifty yards into no man's land, the sergeant demolished one four-man strongpoint with two hand grenades, killing its screaming occupants in almost simultaneous explosions. Before Japanese in a nearby cave could swing their machine gun his way, Julian plunged to cover behind a boulder and emptied his carbine in a single burst, wiping out two more enemy troops.

At that instant, as the Marine got to his knees, another machine gun nest started firing from a position farther up the ridge's steep sides. While comrades on the line covered him with rifle and automatic weapons fire, Julian got to his feet and dashed back for more ammunition to continue the furious one-man assault. Snatching up a satchel of demolitions, a bandoleer of rifle cartridges, and a bazooka, he sprinted back into no man's land.

"You guys stay put until I take care of a few more Nips," he yelled to the platoon, which watched incredulously as Julian went to work.

Three hours later the sergeant still hadn't signaled the troops to move forward. But his intrepid determination had wiped out four more enemy positions, two with demolition charges, one with bazooka fire, and the other with hand grenades. Just when Julian thought the area was cleared enough for the men to advance with a chance of making it alive, a machine gun burst caught him in the chest. He died instantly.

Platoon Sergeant Joseph Julian was now a Marine Corps legend of self-sacrifice and devotion to duty.

On March 14, General Kuribayashi radioed an eloquent message to "the gallant and brave people of Japan," saying:

> **I am pleased to report that we still fight well against the overwhelming material odds of the enemy, and all my officers and men deserve the highest commendation. I humbly apologize to my Emperor that I have failed to live up to expectations and have to yield this key island to the enemy after seeing so many of my officers and men killed.**

On the night of March 21 Kuribayashi sent a final radio message to the garrison on nearby Chichi Jima:

My officers and men are still fighting. The enemy front is two hundred meters from us and they are attacking with flame-throwers and tanks. They have advised us to surrender by leaflets and loudspeakers, but we only laughed at this childish trick.

To all officers and men on Chichi Jima, good-bye.

Sometime in the next few days, apparently, General Kuribayashi committed hara-kiri; and, as was the custom, his aides probably cremated his remains.

On March 26, the last organized resistance ended with an attack by nearly 300 Japanese troops. It occurred shortly before dawn where Army Air Corps crewmen were camped in the central part of the island at Motoyama Airfield Number 2. Just west of the airfield, some antiaircraft soldiers were camped, also, alongside the Seabees. The Fifth Marine Division's Pioneer Battalion, made up largely of black troops, had bivouacked nearby for the night. The black Marines, one of the few such units on Iwo Jima, had finished their shore-party work and were scheduled to leave the island later that day. The Japanese, possibly emerging from underground tunnels, struck quietly from three directions, slashing tent walls and knifing the sleeping airmen.

Marine First Lieutenant Harry L. Martin of Bucyrus, Ohio, of the Fifth Pioneer Battalion, threw up a skirmish line, and his black Marines coolly beat back one attack, then another, by screaming Japanese firing wildly as they came. Lieutenant Martin was wounded twice before he killed four Japanese with his pistol. When the fighting ended some two hours after dawn, the blood-spattered tents yielded forty-four dead airmen and eighty-eight wounded. Strewn about the battleground were 262 Japanese bodies. Eighteen, mostly wounded, were taken prisoner. Thirty-one Marines were wounded, and nine were killed, among them Harry L. Martin, who was killed by a grenade blast as he led the final charge against the enemy. He was awarded the Medal of Honor posthumously.

Thus ended the Battle for Iwo Jima, the bloodiest in Marine Corps history. The entire enemy force of 23,000 defenders had been wiped out, more than 21,000, killed in battle. Only 216 prisoners of war were taken, 34 of them wounded. Marine casualties amounted to 26,575, including 6,126 killed in action. After the battle, Army garrison troops rounded up several hundred stragglers in the last five months of war.

Fleet Admiral Chester W. Nimitz, Commander in Chief, Pacific Fleet, (CINCPAC) said:

> "Among the Americans who fought on Iwo Jima, uncommon valor was a common virtue."

When our unit left Iwo Jima, it never occurred to me to take black, volcanic ash as a souvenir of that island. As we boarded ship to leave that place of such utter death and destruction, we survivors of Iwo Jima were reminded of a little ditty we recited back in those days of the war:

> And when I get to heaven, to Saint Peter I will tell:
> "Another Marine reporting, sir; I've served my time in hell."

Some forty years later, my son Thomas was in the Marines, stationed for a time on Okinawa. Because of a special assignment there, he was unable to go on maneuvers to Iwo Jima with his 3rd Battalion, 9th Marines. However, Tommy asked Link Panettiere, one of his buddies from the same company to do him a favor and bring back some of the volcanic ash for his dad from that island which has now become so famous. Tommy presented the black soil to me when he returned home from the Marines in 1990. I have it on display in my den at home.

In recognition of the performance by LFASCU One on Iwo Jima, our commanding officer, Colonel Vernon E. Megee, was awarded the Legion of Merit on April 25, 1945:

> "For meritorious conduct in action against the enemy from 19 February 1945 to 15 March 1945 while on Iwo Jima, Volcano Islands.
>
> /signed/Holland M. Smith, Lieutenant General, USMC
> Commanding General, Fleet Marine Force, Pacific

Twenty-four years later, in 1969, the United States returned the island of Iwo Jima to Japan. Most bodies of the over 6,000 Marines who died in action there had been removed earlier to the "Punch Bowl" National Memorial Cemetery of the Pacific at Honolulu, Hawaii. Some, of the bodies were transported back to the U. S. mainland for reburial by family request

FIFTH MARINE DIVISION

LOUIS R. LOWERY

Fifth Division cemetery on D-plus twenty-five. Its row on row of crosses, and those in nearby Third and Fourth Division burial grounds, marked the battlefield resting places for 6,821 Marines. Ten years later all bodies were exhumed and returned to American soil for final interment.

Iwo Jima: "Why?" and "How?"

When I was teaching history, a student asked of me:
    "Why take so small an island, isolated, far at sea?"
I told the class what we had done; it jogged my memory.
    At home I wrote that epic down in graphic poetry.

We had to capture Iwo Jima, killing most it's men.
    No other way could it be done, from landing to the end.
It's how I answer inquiries, some fifty years 'tis now;
    And every time I speak of it, I'm wondered by the "how."

With twenty thousand Japanese, and some two thousand more,
    The enemy on Iwo was prepared to fight a war.
They knew that we were coming, and they dug emplacements well,
    To make that island bastion be a place of living hell.

They tunneled deep beneath the rock and black volcanic sand;
    The deepest excavation there was made for high command.
In letters home they said goodbye to friends and family;
    They knew that they would have to die, but with their dignity.

Each promised to keep fighting on until the bitter end;
    That, ere he drew his final breath, he vowed that he'd kill ten.

With no civilians, stubby trees, and weather slightly cold,
    Those eight-square miles of rock and ash were not much to behold.
Why'd such an ugly island, an attraction for us be?
    We had to take an airfield; not just one, or two, but three.

The nineteenth day of February barely saw the sun,
    When warships, in support of landing, fired every gun.

When that barrage had lifted and our planes began to soar,
    Our landing craft with brave Marines went rushing to the shore.
The second, only, time it was in battle history,
    When two Marine divisions landed simultaneously.

The enemy artillery responded with a roar!
    It ripped, and tore, and shattered us, heads down against the shore.
Volcanic ash got soaked with blood; we had no place to hide!
    So move ahead is what we did, with pain . . . and "Semper Pride."

By nightfall we had fought across a half a mile of land:
    Two thousand men, our dead and wounded, scattered on the sand.

The next three days we made advances, front and to the rear;
    But February twenty-third, a sight we had to cheer:
Five-hundred-foot Mount Suribachi, highest ground there'd be
    Was captured! There our flag was raised . . . for all Marines to see.

A most dramatic moment then! And, why had it been done?
    Was that the end of fighting? And was the battle won?
No, for bitter war continued on the battlefield below;
    Such fierce resistance plaguing us: Another month to go.

About that time, to fill a gap, give weary troops a lift,
    The 3rd Marine Division came to join the 4th and 5th.
And now, with three Marine divisions lined up to the north,
    The enemy began to feel our might as we moved forth.

With two thirds of the island left; and they, entrenched uphill,
    Surrender was not in their plan: More blood would have to spill.
No matter what we threw at them, resistance was so hard,
    Each day's advances had to be just measured by the yard.

Marines were falling left and right, but we could still give thanks,
    As battlefield replacements joined our now-depleted ranks.

The enemy was losing ground, as we pursued for days,
    Relentlessly attacking a variety of ways.
We called in air support so close that we could feel the heat,
    As burning napalm dropped ahead of us, three hundred feet.

We burned them out! We sealed their caves. Some fighting hand to hand.

On March the fourth, a big B-29 came in to land.

It needed help, just halfway home, some seven hundred miles;
    The crewmen knelt and kissed the ground, their faces bathed in smiles.

Repairs were made in record time; big plane flew on its way:
    'Twas back to Saipan's bomber base to fly another day.
In five months some two thousand more such rescues would be made;
    Each Army flying crew of ten was grateful to be saved.

The rate that men on Iwo fell was one for every minute.
    Presented graphically, there's yet another way to put it:
When seven men would fall, 'twas like a seven-minute scene:
    Three dead were theirs. One dead was ours. Three wounded were Marine.

In general, fighting took four weeks; some units, more like five.
    Yes, we survivors, boarding ship, thanked God to be alive.

It was our only victory with casualties more then they:
    The dead and wounded on that island, unbelievable to say.
Their dead, in thousands: twenty-one; and ours: six thousand, not alive.
    The total of our dead and wounded, in the thousands: twenty-five.

We men of Iwo reminisce,
        Some fifty years 'tis now:
            Of lost Marines;
                No tougher fight.
                     We know the "why,"
                       The "how."

Frank Gardner

(Written in 1987, when, in retirement, I did some substitute teaching.)

JOSEPH JULIAN: Marine Corps Legend

One Joseph "Rudy" Julian,
  A World War Two Marine,
Was killed on Iwo Jima in
  A most heroic scene.

Before he went to battlefields
  He went to visit home;
He knew that seas and islands were
  The places he would roam.

Back home in Massachusetts
  He then told his family
That, after fighting enemy,
  Alive, he might not be.

He told his pastor and his friends,
  When on his way to war,
That he would stand up for the things
  We all were fighting for.

On Iwo Jima, "forty-five,"
  Where 3 Marine divisions fought,
The enemy would fight to death,
  And vowed not to be caught.

So, this was where Joe Julian
  Would lead his band of men;
They knew the way to fight, and he
  Would tell them where and when.

On nineteenth day of battle,
  The platoon by Joe was led;
He told his men to cover him
  While he went on ahead.

Because they were receiving fire
  From several cliff-side caves,
Their chief went forward, covered by
  The firing from his braves.

For three full hours he stayed out front
  With weapons for the job:
Bazooka; rifle; with grenades
  He knew just how to lob.

He knocked out six of their positions
  For his men's advance;
He was about to signal them,
  But never got the chance.

A well-concealed machine gun fired
  And struck him in the chest!
His death was instantaneous;
  His men had lost their best.

Platoon Sergeant Joseph Julian,
  Marine Corps legend now:
He didn't order men out front;
  He simply showed them how.

*Joseph Julian was awarded
the Congressional Medal of Honor,
posthumously.*

Frank Gardner

CHAPTER 14

*   *   *

Two Weeks between Battles

On March 15, 1945, LFASCU One, and two other units of equal size were pulled off Iwo Jima while the fighting was still in progress. We had

Butch, a loyal, alert, Doberman Pinscher stands guard in a sandy foxhole as his handler snatches a few well-earned minutes of rest on Iwo Jima.

to make it down to Saipan, 700 miles south, to join the fleet headed toward the next invasion. One group was a Joint Assault Signal Company (JASCO). The other, was a war-dog platoon that we had seen several times during the battle, out on patrol with sleek, black Doberman Pinschers. This was probably the 6th War Dog Platoon, attached to the Fifth Marine Division for Iwo Jima. Now it would take its logical place with the new Sixth Marine Division. The Joint Assault Signal

Company was probably the 1st JASCO, attached to the Fourth Marine Division for Iwo Jima. Now it would take its logical place with the First Marine Division for the next invasion. We three units had to get ready for another landing, on the "larger island" we had heard about back at Ewa.

We were the first ground units to leave Iwo Jima as viable organizations. Perhaps another unit or two, such as a rocket battalion or an artillery observation squadron, could have also left Iwo early to take part in the next invasion. If so, it would have been on another ship, and certainly, within the next day or two in order to join the new invasion convoy.

I, along with about fifty enlisted men of LFASCU One, went down to the beach that day and boarded LST-84 while the battle still raged in the northern heights of the island. Our drivers, Whittaker and Merle maneuvered our several vehicles, including our bulldozer, from the beach onto the huge bow-ramp and up to the open-air, topside deck of the ship.

In the above photograph taken on that occasion, we are shown, left to right, standing: Milton Urban, Robert Thompson, Frank Gardner, Herman Mastrogiovanni, and Al Buff; kneeling, Bill Staats, John Bartley, and Bill Herrman. All of us were radio operators.

With all men, equipment, and war dogs loaded, our LST shoved off immediately, cruising due south toward Saipan. The next four days we relaxed and caught up on our laundry, using salt-water soap. Because this type ship rode so much lower in the water, some of us used a simpler method of washing or rinsing heavier items, such as dungarees and blankets. We secured them to ropes and tossed them overboard where they benefited from the speedy agitation of the ocean water. (For full view of an LST, see Page 192.)

On March 19, we arrived at Saipan, where we debarked and off-loaded our motorized equipment at Tanapag Harbor. We spent the next week getting ready for the new campaign. One notable routine was that every morning we all had to line up to take our medicine. Our corpsman, John Church, gave us Atabrine tablets to swallow. These were to guard against malaria on the next, still unknown, island. We would take Atabrine for the next three months.

(Written on Saipan)

March 23, 1945

Dear Mother:

For the last few days I have been very busy. At Iwo Jima, we boarded an LST for a rear area. We had a pleasant trip and came ashore on this island, which is beautiful, and happens to be the same one I was on last summer.

We've been working hard here, as we have to shove off very soon—so soon, in fact, that this will be my last letter for some time.

Today I got off for a short time to visit some Spanish friends I made on my last visit here. They are doing fine and certainly were glad to see me.

When I get mail, it's all in batches. I received a month-and-a-half's newspapers when I landed here.

Enclosed is a picture of some of us on the LST. Can you pick me out?

The photograph I sent home was taken on the LST several days after we departed Iwo Jima, approaching Saipan where the weather was warmer.

I am in the center of back row, between men sitting on jeeps. Herman Mastrogiovanni is leaning against the jeep on the left.

At that point in the Pacific War, three Marine divisions of the 5th Amphibious Corps were still involved in the battle on Iwo Jima. The three other Marine divisions, under 3rd Amphibious Corps, were headed for the new invasion. The Fleet Marine Force was fully involved in two different operations at the same time.

In my March 23 letter, the part about visiting "Spanish friends," was to let mother know that I had seen Sister Angelica Salaverria.

When I saw Sister on Saipan, I told her I had just come from Iwo Jima and I would have to leave shortly on another mission. Although I couldn't give her any further details, I'm sure she suspected that I was on my way to another invasion.

Following my visit with sister, she sent a letter in English to my mother:

Missionary Sisters of Mercy
C/O Civil Affairs Section, Saipan
15 April 1945

My dear Mrs. Gardner:

I was so pleased to receive your kind letter with its pleasant news. Several days ago I began to answer you but before I finished my letter Francis came to see us. So I am going to write again telling you something about him. We all were so glad to meet him again. He is in fine health, but I found him different and sad. I am very sorry to tell you this, but I can not suffer to hide it to you, because you can help him so much with your letters and your prayers. However, I would not like he could realize that I have communicated you this, so that if he should write me he could be able to do freely. He promised to write, if he does, I think I will be able to help him with the grace of God. We all pray for him very much.

I know that this letter cannot give you so much pleasure as the first one, but I know too, that you will thank me as much as the first time. Is it not true? But do not worry too much, please. You know to see the kind hand of God in all your things, and I am sure that you know to make profit of this pain too. Now it will be good for you to remember the verse that you wrote me: "My life is but a weaving."

You said that you have two of our pictures. According to the signs that you gave me I think I will be in the center. The wound was caused by a bullet which entered the right side and went out the back, but I am perfectly well now.

How much we thank you for your prayers. Please give our thanks to Sisters also and tell them to continue praying because we need so much.

You wrote me that you would like to send me something. Thank you very much. I would like to have a missal in Spanish by Dom Gaspar Lefevre translation of P. German del Prado. I will be very glad if you can get me one.

I am glad for your vacation. I think you have found many interesting things in Cuba and you have had opportunity to speak Spanish.

Please do not forget us before your little Infant Jesus of Prague.

Sincerely yours in Christ

Angelica Salaverria

Mother made the following pencil notation on the back of the letter:

"The verse Sister refers to is one I sent her in connection with all she and the other sisters have been through."

My life is but a weaving

Between my God and me.
I may but choose the colors,
He worketh steadily.
Full oft He weaveth sorrow,
And I in foolish pride,
Forget He sees the upper,
And I the under side.

From the end of the war in 1945 until 1950, mother and I kept in touch with Sister Angelica Salaverria, first on Saipan and later, after she was transferred to the island of Truk, in the Carolines. In addition to letters, we exchanged Christmas cards and donated money to the missions of the Sisters of Mercy on both of those islands.

Shown on the next page is a photograph of LST 1097, anchored off Okinawa in 1945.

Andrew Savage donated the photograph by way of the Internet. His father-in-law had served aboard LST 1097 at Okinawa in 1945. (LST stands for Landing Ship, Tank.)

CHAPTER 15

*   *   *

Okinawa

LFASCU One boarded the *USS Bladen*, APA 63, at Tanapag Harbor, Saipan. On March 27, 1945, we weighed anchor, heading west from the Marianas in a huge convoy of ships. We learned that the larger island we were going to invade was called Okinawa, in the Ryukyu chain. It was 300 miles south of Kyushu, one of the main home islands of Japan. The number of ships involved in this operation came to 1,457, making it the largest cross-ocean fleet in history, before or since that time.

INVASION OF OKINAWA
1 APRIL 1945

It was called Operation Iceberg, to be carried out in the Central Pacific Area. Therefore, it would be under the overall command of Fleet Admiral Chester W. Nimitz, Commander in Chief of Pacific Ocean Areas (CINCPOA). The ground forces would comprise a field army, the only time such a large land force was used in the Central Pacific during the war.

Compared with the Solomons, New Guinea, and the Philippines, Okinawa was a much smaller island. However, it was the largest island of all those we invaded in the Central Pacific Area. It is four times larger than Saipan, being 67 miles long and measuring from three to ten miles wide. It had a civilian population of more than 200,000. About 60,000 persons lived in its capital city, Naha. The island's garrison of defenders numbered well over 100,000 men.

The ground forces for Operation Iceberg would consist of four Army infantry divisions at 16,000 men, each; and three Marine Divisions at 19,000 men, each. They were organized, as follows:

TENTH ARMY
General Simon Bolivar Buckner, U. S. Army

Twenty-fourth Army Corps	*Third Amphibious Corps*
Major General John R. Hodge, U.S. Army	Major General Roy S. Geiger USMC
7th Infantry Division: Land on Love Day	1st Marine Division: Land on Love Day
96th Infantry Division: Land on Love Day	6th Marine Division: Land on Love Day
77th Infantry Division: ***To land, L-minus-5, on nearby Kerama Retto islands and provide artillery support for main landings on Okinawa.***	2nd Marine Division: ***Demonstrate fake landing at southern coast to divert attention from actual west coast landing beaches on Love Day.***
27th Infantry Division: Floating reserve	

The invasion of Okinawa had been scheduled, originally, for late March 1945. Because this would be so soon after Iwo Jima, the naval officers at Makalapa wanted to avoid confusion in their planning deliberations. They decided to use two different "Day" designations for the separate invasions. The usual designation of "D-Day" was assigned to the first of the two invasions, Iwo Jima's Operation Detachment. For the second invasion, Okinawa's Operation Iceberg, "L" for "Landing" was chosen. However, neither "L" nor "Landing" would be spoken as such. What we heard used was "Love Day," referring to our phonetic alphabet for the letter "L."

Years later, during the 1970s, my daughter Lorraine served in the US. Army. She told me that the phonetic alphabet for our Armed Forces has been improved. Most of the one-syllable words we had used in World War II were replaced with words having two syllables. All the words became more identifiable. So, "Love" was changed to "Lima." Our old, "Able, Baker, Charlie, Dog" became the new, "Alpha, Bravo, Charlie, Delta."

For obvious reasons, during World War II we had used the letter "D" rather than our phonetic "Dog," in referring to the many D-Days we had in the Pacific; and about six in the European Theater of Operations, including the largest D-Day at Normandy.

Again, as had been the case on Iwo Jima, our Air Support Control Unit would be assigned to a Marine Amphibious Corps. We would provide close air support for the three Marine divisions. The other Marine Air Support Control Units, numbers Two and Three, would be assigned to the Tenth Army and the 24th Army Corps respectively.

Love Day on Okinawa occurred on Easter Sunday, April Fools Day, April 1, 1945. It was the strangest major landing of American troops in the Central Pacific. We landed practically unopposed on the lower western beaches. Our small unit, for the first time, was able to land on the day of invasion. By nightfall the American beachhead was about nine miles wide and three miles deep, including Kadena and Yonton Airfields. More than 60,000 men of the four assault divisions were ashore, and 15,000 more support and service troops had landed. The Fourth Marine Regiment, of the Sixth Marine Division, sustained only two men killed and nine wounded by isolated enemy snipers on Love Day.

Ironically, the most Marine casualties on that day were sustained by troops who did not land on the island. LST-884, carrying Marines of the Second Division, was in convoy thirty miles south of Okinawa in the early morning hours of April 1, 1945, when a Japanese *kamikaze* airplane struck it at the water line. The warplane slammed into a compartment where 15 Marines were killed almost instantly from the impact and the airplane's burning engine. Eleven other men were killed and twenty wounded, including Marines and Navy crewmen.

The order was given to abandon ship for fear that the vessel, laden down with TNT and gasoline, might explode, killing all persons aboard. Many Marines and sailors jumped overboard. In the next day or two, many of them were rescued, either at sea or on nearby deserted islets. When the fires finally went out on LST-884, some crewmen went back aboard the ship. They learned that the two bombs carried by the *kamikaze* had failed to explode, or else there might have been no survivors at all.

Kamikaze in Japanese means "divine wind," the term given to a typhoon in the year 1281 that destroyed Kublai Khan's Mongol invasion fleet headed for Japan.

On Sunday morning, April 1, 1945, the rest of the Second Marine Division went ahead with its planned demonstration of a fake landing at the far southeast coast. Within a few days it was apparent that the division would not be needed to secure the northern portion of Okinawa; so it was sent back to its base camp on Saipan. The high command would thus have a fully intact Marine division available to spearhead the invasion of Japan scheduled for later in 1945.

The enemy's use of the *kamikaze* had developed about six months earlier. By October 1944, the Japanese naval air fleet had been almost wiped out by American Navy fighter pilots. At that time, with its dwindling naval air power, the enemy tried a new tactic in a desperate attempt to attack American warships. Admiral Takijiro Onishi, commander of the Japanese 1st Air Fleet in the Philippines, recruited the first *kamikaze* pilots. He proposed the first suicide mission on October 19 to two of his squadrons. Every pilot volunteered. The Admiral felt that airplanes with bombs crash-diving on our ships would be the surest way to sink our ships.

From their inception, on October 19, 1944, through January 13, 1945, *kamikazes* succeeded in attacking 128 vessels, mostly in the Philippines in late 1944. Most of the ships attacked were damaged, including 17 aircraft carriers and five battleships; a few smaller ships or vessels were sunk. However, the U. S. Navy kept the enemy's new tactic a secret, and no accounts of the Japanese *kamikaze* attacks appeared in the American press during the war.

After early successes in the Philippines, the idea of using *kamikazes* was extended to the Central Pacific. The Japanese began training young men specifically for such suicide missions. In the last year of the war, some 5,000 volunteers had been trained at a special base on Japan's southernmost home island of Kyushu. Many were teenagers from high school or college. They never received flight training. Instead, using dummy models on the ground, they were given only rudimentary instructions as to accelerating for take off, staying airborne, and moving the control stick to guide the plane and follow an accomplished leader pilot. Apparently, most of them were not taught how to land the airplane.

When their turn came to strike our fleet, a selected group mounted bomb-laden warplanes and took off for the first time. After following a leader to target areas, they knew only how to aim their flying explosives down and into American warships. The *kamikaze* flyers knew they were on suicide missions; however, they believed that life after death was assured by sacrificing themselves on earth for their emperor.

In February and March 1945, some *kamikaze* attacks occurred off Iwo Jima, damaging several ships and inflicting about 2,000 casualties on U. S. Navy personnel. It was off Okinawa, however, from April to June 1945, that these suicide pilots made their greatest impact on our fleet during the Second World War.

The enemy strategy on Okinawa became clear very early in the battle. While we were attempting to enlarge our beachhead, they planned to attack our fleet with *kamikazes*, to sink as many of our ships as possible, and drive away the others. Then their superior numbers of fighting troops, over 110,000, could descend on our 75,000 men ashore and annihilate us on the beaches before we could land any more reinforcements.

The Japanese strategy didn't work. Our Navy fought off the daily, incessant *kamikaze* raids from the Japanese homeland. Most of the inexperienced enemy fliers were shot down by our carrier pilots or by anti-aircraft fire from the fleet.

Meanwhile, ashore, the First Marine Division held the central portion of the island and its two large airfields, Yonton and Kadena. The Army's two infantry divisions, the 7th and the 96th, turned south. Within a few days they came up against the main concentration of enemy troops. The defenders were entrenched in the formidable Machinato Line across the lower neck of the island.

The Sixth Marine Division turned north and began pursuing a Japanese division into the rugged mountainous terrain in that part of the island. My outfit went along with the fast moving 6th Division to provide close air support.

The Army's 27th Infantry Division was still being held in floating reserve. Because of continuing *kamikaze* attacks on our ships, the division had to be landed without further delay. On April 9, the 27th landed and went into reserve for the 24th Army Corps in the southern part of the island.

By mid-April, Major General John R. Hodge, commander of the 24th
Corps, needed more troops to overcome
the stiffening enemy resistance in the
south. So, on April 15, he moved the 27th
Infantry Division from reserve into the
center of the front line. He now had three
infantry divisions arrayed against the
enemy's Machinato Line.

By the time we began writing home,
our officers informed us that, as at Iwo,
we could again divulge the name of the
island in our letters:

Okinawa
April 12, 1945

Dear Mother:
   This island is very different from anything else I've seen
in the Pacific. There are many small towns and villages, farms,
broken down thatched huts, and many evergreen trees. The
weather is still cold.
   The battle for us in the Marine Corps has been amazingly
different from any other. We are more mechanized, and employ
wider movements.
   Down south, the Army Corps has run into a stone wall
lately. To exhibit the difference between this and Iwo, note that
here, in the first 24 hours, the Marine Corps troops secured
an area greater than Iwo Jima, including one airfield.
   The rain made it miserable for us a couple of days ago.

Enemy air activity has been much more intense than at Saipan or Iwo. Whereas on those two operations the planes came over mostly at night, here they come over all day and all night.

There is not as much trouble from the civilians here as at Saipan. As we moved up 15 miles last week along the roads, I noticed some of them still working in the fields. At other points they were gathering for refuge at our civil affairs camps.

By the way, something I forgot to mention in my last letter: Congratulations on your promotion from ensign to lieutenant junior grade.

*   *   *

Okinawa
April 20, 1945

Dear Mary:

I presume mother has already told you of my being here on Okinawa.

I received your lovely Easter card in the mail yesterday; also, a letter from two of Dorothy's 4th grade pupils. They told me how much they loved Dorothy and how they had been praying for me. Dottie added a small note at the bottom.

Mother writes quite regularly, short but interesting letters. She told me of all the prayers offered for the Marines on Iwo.

> *Okinawa is a large island compared to any others in the Central Pacific west of Hawaii. It's in a more temperate climate than Saipan. For the Marines, so far, it's been a comparatively easy operation. Our landing was practically unopposed; and in our sweep northward from the beaches we have been chasing the Japs all over this portion of the island.*
>
> *Enemy air activity has been quite intense. Being so close to the Japanese homeland, Shanghai, and Formosa, we hardly miss a day that we don't have from two to five air raids. On one day there were twenty raids in a matter of four hours. The strikes seem to be directed more toward the airfields and the landing beaches down in the central part of the island. Since leaving that area, we have not been bothered so much, for we are now in rugged, hilly country, and it affords good camouflage. We have, however, seen a couple of exciting dogfights overhead.*
>
> *Our camp is situated on a grassy meadow that drops off in jagged coral cliffs into the China Sea. The swimming is good where I have found an excellent coral pool, deep and clear. When not on duty, I go there to wash my clothes and myself, and spend pleasant afternoons in the sun, searching for seashells.*

From our campsite, we could look out to the China Sea at the small, offshore island of Ie Shima, where the 77th Infantry Division landed on April 16. Two days later, Ernie Pyle, the famous civilian war correspondent, who had followed the Army earlier in North Africa and Europe, was killed while covering his first battle in the Pacific. He was buried on Ie Shima in the 77th Division cemetery. That island was secured quickly by the 77th in a matter of six days.

In addition to the job of maintaining radio communications with our forward observers on the ground and our air coordinator flying above the battlefield, we radio operators took our turns recording the conversations between our coordinator and the pilots on station for air strikes. Tape recording technology was not available to us during the war, so we listened with earphones and typed out the voice messages we heard over the radio. To double-check each other, at least two radio operators were monitoring the same radio channel. When he spoke, each pilot used his airplane's identifying number, which, of course, was most important for us to record.

Previously, on Iwo Jima, we had performed our noisy typing inside the Combat Information Center (CIC), somewhat to the distraction of our land-based pilots and other officers who were using their several radios for two-way communication. On Okinawa, the system was improved. A huge trailer on wheels was parked outside the CIC with a dozen counter-desks, each having a radio receiver, set of earphones, and typewriter. That's where we radio operators recorded the radio conversations involving air strikes. When on duty, eight or ten of us might be pounding away on our typewriters at the same time.

Since we were well behind the front line, and there was no threat of enemy artillery, we did not have to dig foxholes. We merely pitched pup tents by putting two shelter halves together. An officer was attacked in his tent one night, by an enemy straggler while we slept. A Japanese soldier was surprised while searching for food in the officer's tent, and slashed the young pilot across the face. The assailant was quickly subdued and taken away as a prisoner of war.

By April 20, the 6th Marine Division had beaten the Japanese forces in northern Okinawa, ending all organized resistance in that portion of the island. We had a week of rest, during which time I served as lifeguard for our outfit as we relaxed along the shore and swam in the China Sea.

In my April 24 letter, shown on the two next pages, I described military currency issued to us for Okinawa. It is displayed in my photo album at home. Photos of it are shown following the letter.

Photographs of Okinawan civilians are shown on the page after the military currency. One photo shows some elderly refugees, moving past a Marine sentry. The other shows an orphan boy, sharing a foxhole with two Marines.

Okinawa
April 24, 1945

Dear Mother:

We have now settled down to a permanent camp. It is situated near a large grassy meadow, surrounded by pine trees. Of course, we are bivouacked in the pines for camouflage. One edge of the meadow drops off in jagged coral cliffs to the China Sea. Near this point there is a Japanese shrine, wherein two stone upright pillars support a horizontal one at the top. Nearby is a stone table with stone benches circled around it.

Down at the water's edge there are some very deep and clear pools formed in the coral. They are wonderful for swimming, but the rocks are sharp, so I wear shoes in the water. I wash my clothes there and spend pleasant sunny afternoons off duty swimming and searching for shells among the rocks.

We get the news every day. We heard about President Roosevelt's death on April 12 and the news of our great victories in Germany. We got word last night of the Russian Army's entry into Berlin, and of the imminent junction between the Russian and American armies. We feel good about it over here because we know that we'll get a lot of help now.

You have probably noticed the return address on the envelope.

(S/Sgt. F. V. Gardner, USMC
LFASCU #1, 3rd Phib Corps
FMF PAC; F. P. O.
San Francisco, California)

It doesn't mean that I'm in a new outfit. It doesn't mean anything except that we have finally come around to having a mailing address the same as our true identity. The LFASCU #1 means: "Landing Force, Air Support Control Unit Number One." We have been LFASCU #1 ever since we left Oahu in January. Of course, you know what the Third Amphibious Corps is. Awhile back we were under a different corps.

Before landing here, we had to turn in our American currency for "invasion" money: 20 yen for $2.00; 10 yen for $1.00; 5 yen: 50 cents; 1 yen: 10 cents; 50 sen: 5 cents; and 10 sen: one cent. I'm not sure whether there are any 1 sen notes; but, if so, that would equal one mill, wouldn't it?

My time's getting short, so I'll close now and write again before too long.

Marines share foxhole with young Okinawan whose parents have died in the fighting.

Okinawan refugees.

(Shown here, from my photo album, is Japanese currency I found in an abandoned farmhouse on the battlefield.)

At the end of April, after having secured nearby Ie Shima, the 77th Division came over to join the main battle. General Buckner now had six divisions in his Tenth Army on Okinawa. Four were Army infantry divisions; two were Marine divisions. He could now re-juggle his lineup at the southern front.

The 96th Division, which had been badly mauled, was pulled out of the line for a well-deserved rest. The newly arrived 77th Division replaced it on the right flank. The 7th Division, which had not been so severely tested, remained on the left flank. The 27th Division was pulled out of the center and sent north for general garrison duty. The 77th Division then adjusted to the center and the right flank was taken over by the well rested 1st Marine Division.

A week later, the American advance was slowed by ferocious enemy resistance at the Shuri Line. The 6th Marine Division came south and moved into place on the far right of the line. The 77th Infantry Division and the 1st Marine Division then adjusted in the center. General Buckner now had four divisions attacking the Shuri Line. On the left, were the 7th and 77th Infantry Divisions of the 24th Army Corps. On the right, were the 1st and 6th Marine Divisions of the Third Amphibious Corps.

LFASCU One also moved south to provide close air support to the Third Amphibious Corps and its two Marine divisions at the Shuri Line. We packed up the heavier clothing we had used on Iwo Jima. This included extra blankets and the wind-breaker-type field jackets we had needed in the colder climate. We included some souvenirs and trinkets, which we had collected as we advanced through the northern part of the island. We tagged our sea bags with our names and LFASCU #1, to be sent to Marine Corps Air Station at Ewa, Oahu.

When we returned to Ewa after Okinawa, an attendant at the mail depot told us that our sea bags had never been received there. So, we assumed that our gear had gone down with a transport ship, sunk by either a Japanese submarine or a *kamikaze* in May 1945.

With the loss of those souvenirs, the only large item I brought back from Okinawa was a conch shell I had picked up on the beach. I have it in our family room at home. Also, I brought back some Japanese yen notes, which are now displayed in my album from the war. They are shown on the previous page.

In our trip down to the southern half of the island around May 1, 1945, most of our men rode in large troop-transport trucks. I drove a jeep with four men as passengers. At our new camp, we were issued large canvass garrison tents that could accommodate four men. The first couple of nights we were bitten by huge fire ants. So a few of us scrounged some litters or stretchers from a nearby graves registration supply depot. We had to sort through a pile of bloodied stretchers to pick out those that were fairly clean. We took them to our tent and used them as cots, raising them off the ground with sandbags. To guard against the pesky ants, we placed the legs of the stretchers in small cans half filled with kerosene.

Okinawa
May 10, 1945

Dear Mother:

Well, we have picked up and moved from our former campsite. There's a little bit more activity where we are now.

Up where we were before, we even got a chance to put on a minstrel show that we had rehearsed three or four days. I was an MP: "Minstrel Police."

We saw some high-ranking Navy and Marine Corps officers a while back. I was surprised to see an added star on one of the generals.

Things are rather monotonous right now but will start popping fairly soon.

---

*   *   *

> *Okinawa*
> *May 13, 1945*
>
> *Dear Mary:*
> *You probably have already seen the last letter I sent to mother, so you know I've moved. I guess the newspaper gives you more dope than I could.*
> *Censorship regulations are somewhat strict for our outfit. We can't mention the name of the operation we were on before this one. We're one of the very few outfits here that were there.*
> *The air raids still come thick and fast. You have probably read of the Japanese special attack force. The Tokyo radio sometimes refers to them as "the Japanese one-way runners." The Tokyo radio says that our fleet is practically on the bottom of the ocean. I guess they think that every suicide plane they send out sinks his assigned ship.*
> *When is mother's birthday, July 11 or July 6? I was thinking that it'd be a good idea to send flowers. What do you think? Do you have any better ideas?*

In one of mother's letters, she asked about AWS-5 being among those units that received the Presidential Unit Citation for action on Saipan. In the following letter, I explained to her why only part of my old outfit had been included.

Okinawa
May 22, 1945

Dear Mother:

Yesterday I received some back mail from April. It must've gotten detoured somewhere along the line.

About that citation, Col. Sampson is partially right. You see, on Saipan our outfit was split up into three sections, one to the corps and the other two to each of the two Marine divisions. The Fourth Marine Division received the citation for Saipan. Those from AWS-5, who were attached to it, were included. (The 2nd Division had already received it for Tarawa.) *There is some talk, however, that such a small outfit cannot receive an award for only part of its men, and they say that the rest of us might get it yet. ***

It's really news to me about Mary's vocation. I had almost gathered as much for some time, but she never mentioned it to me. Does she want to teach like Dorothy? Will she go through St. Joseph's Seminary?

The rain is getting bad around here lately. The weather is getting warmer too. I think I'm beginning to turn yellow from all the Atabrine I've been taking.

Enclosed you will find $20.00 that I want you to put aside for me. That makes $100 now, doesn't it?

Have you heard any more about the Pearl Harbor assignment lately, or have you changed your mind?** I think you really want to take it from all the talking you do about it, but you seem to be afraid to venture forth. Am I right?

I think I'd still like to get into the Navy's V-12 program when I get back to the Mount. ** Maybe we could check with Father Cogan on that.

I'm signing off now to go on watch.

---

*   The rest of us from old AWS-5 never received the Presidential Unit Citation.

** Neither Mother's possible assignment to Pearl Harbor, nor my joining V-12, ever developed because the war ended so soon thereafter.

Below the hillside, across the small creek from our camp, quite a few soldiers from an Army outfit had pitched their pup tents right down near the running water. This would turn out to be a mistake for them, but at times I used to envy them the lazy life they had. They could scoop up water so close by for washing. They were able to cook right outside their tents and rinse off their mess kits in the free, rushing water within arm's reach.

Okinawa, May 27, 1945

Dear Mother:

The rain here lately has been bad. Yesterday we had quite a flood in the draw below our camp. A dam had washed out further upstream. The flood hit suddenly, as I was coming off a wicked tour of all-night guard duty in a driving rain, the like of which none of us had ever seen before.

It was an eventful night. The thing that made it so, aside from all the rain, was a little scare we received from the Army camp on the other side of our hill. Along about midnight, a bunch of Doggies started firing at something. What was going on, none of us ventured to find out.

We hadn't had any such excitement for some time, and the front lines by now are far away. Things like large bodies of enemy troops popping up this far behind the lines are rare, but not altogether unheard of, as a certain Seabee camp found out the other night when the Army drove a pocket of Nips into their area. There aren't any such pockets around here for miles. So we soon dismissed any fears we had and concentrated on keeping dry for the rest of the night.

From two to six in the morning the monsoon struck. After breakfast a group of us took shovels and went wading. The culvert under the main road, which should have taken care of the water, was clogged with debris and oil drums, and the road ended up a foot under water. We set to work digging gullies on the other side of the road to let the water drain off down the bank.

Oil drums, water cans, lumber and all kinds of gear from the Army camp washed into the wide draw below us. A lot of Doggie pup tents were washed away. It reminded me of the Potomac River at Great Falls above Washington. I saw soldiers wallowing around, shoulder-deep, in vain attempts to salvage personal gear and supplies. One Jeep was up to the windshield in water, and a DUKW vehicle was trying to pull it out. Other Jeeps and trucks were left standing in their semi-submerged condition. A supply tent with a few hundred new Army blankets and miscellaneous gear was washed out.

The water finally drained off when we unclogged the culvert. We had managed to salvage some personal gear belonging to the soldiers. We returned an expensive Leica camera to a soldier named Dempsey. The remainder of the day the unfortunate Doggies toiled to move their camp up to the crest of their hill.

*   *   *

Okinawa

June 2, 1945

Dear Mary:

The time has been long since my last letter. It's been rather busy lately. Heavy rains have made things very difficult.

We've had two days of good weather, now, and things are looking better all over, especially in the front lines.

I have two letters here that I've been carrying around for some time, waiting for the chance to answer them. The mail has been coming in a little slower now. Two weeks ago it came very fast, due to late mail from the old address and fresh mail from the new, hitting us all at once.

(See letter, dated April 24, 1945, about the change in return address.)

In your letter of May 9, you mentioned wonderful news. I can't recall any great drives we had around that time. I know there were general advances. Someday I'll check up on all these letters and their misunderstandings. That will have to come from the other end of the line. I don't save any of the letters I receive.

(Today {1998} I'm sure Mary's "wonderful news" was about Germany's surrender on May 7, 1945.)

Lately, things are going well in the battle, which is no great news to the Japs, should they intercept this letter.

Tokyo Radio reports: "The fate of the Japanese Empire rests with the Battle of Okinawa, which is rapidly reaching a climax."

As far as chemistry goes, I'm afraid I wouldn't be of much help with aromatic ketones or aldehydes.

I'm glad you have finally seen the inside of our chapel at the Mount.

Recently I've seen a few good movies, including, "Princess O'Roarke" and "Gaslight."

*　　*　　*

Okinawa
June 4, 1945

Dear Mother:

After a week of rain, we had a two-day let up, and we really made some good advances against the enemy. Now it's raining again all day today. We're expecting a typhoon to hit the island very soon.

No, that woman whose son is in a ground crew will probably get home when she says. For aviation outfits, the usual time is 14 months. For "bastard" units such as ours, attached to a different Corps for each operation, you can never tell.

Regarding snakes, I've only seen a few. Remember all the horrible animals and reptiles, Saipan was supposed to have? It's never as bad as it sounds. There are rats here, and they're a nuisance.

Our regular duties included radio communications and recording air-ground conversations by day, plus occasional night watches in the CIC. In addition, we radio operators took turns at nighttime guard duty at the perimeter of our camp. One night while on such duty at the hilltop above our camp, I experienced an emotional and deeply spiritual awareness. The rains had ended. It was a quiet, clear night in June 1945. The stars filled the heavens above me. I was alone with only my rifle and my thoughts.

I reflected on the thousands of men already killed on Okinawa. I knew the enemy had lost men numbering in the tens of thousands. Even though the rate of our men killed in action was much lower, it was still in the thousands. Each battalion and regiment submitted daily casualty reports up through both divisions. These were compiled and distributed to all units by Third Corps headquarters. If I didn't see those reports on my occasional night watches in the CIC, I had a daily reminder fairly near our camp. I would see those bloody stretchers continue to pile up outside the graves registration headquarters.

I had survived Saipan and Iwo Jima, the two toughest battles before this one in the Central Pacific. Now, this struggle was even worse. How long could the maiming, the devastation, and the killing go on? If I survived this battle, there would be the ultimate onslaught when we next invaded Japan.

On that lonely hilltop, I asked God why so many Marines had to die. Why was I being spared? I was overcome with emotion. With no one nearby to hear my anguish, I broke down and cried. I suppose I had held my feelings within for too long. Now was the opportunity to release them, at least to myself. I cried aloud for a couple of minutes. The tears washed over my face.

Then, when I recovered my emotions, I prayed to God for peace and resolve to make my life worthwhile. I told God that if I survived this island battle and the invasion of Japan, I would return home and devote myself to the service of my country in peacetime.

Forty years later, in Falls Church, Virginia, June 1985, I wrote a poem (Page 229) about this "Vow on Okinawa."

Okinawa
June 10, 1945

Dear Mother:
Well, the battle here is rapidly coming to a close. We have the enemy retreating fast now. They might not be able to turn and make a last-ditch stand.
We've been enjoying clear weather for a while. Because of this, we have been able to deliver some good close air support. This greatly helped our latest advances.

There were times we had less to do when no squadrons were on station to make air strikes. One day during such a lull in activity, we received a radio call from an unscheduled Navy squadron. The pilots had been out over the ocean most of that day, doing picket duty for the fleet. The squadron leader reported that he and his fliers were on their way back to their carrier with a full load of bombs and torpedoes. Since they had not found any enemy ships to attack, they wondered if we might supply some likely targets. Otherwise, they would have to jettison their bombs into the sea before landing on their carrier.

It appeared this squadron was not very adept at close air support. However, our CIC officer in charge agreed reluctantly on an air strike. The air coordinator was apprised of the situation and indicated that he would lead them against some simple targets. He had them follow him on the usual "dummy run." They all acknowledged they had seen the landmark river running east and west, with the enemy targets on the southern side.

As they circled back 360 degrees to do the "live run," the slower, more cumbersome torpedo bombers swung too wide. They became separated from the faster fighters and dive-bombers. The leading torpedo bomber saw a river running east and west, so he crossed it and unleashed his explosives on the other side. Unfortunately, it was a river behind our lines. The target he hit was a Navy camp of Seabees. Two or three other planes, following close behind him, also dropped their bombs.

I was on duty at the time. Within a few seconds I heard a desperate voice over the radio, screaming, "Stop the strike! Stop the strike!" I continued typing everything I heard on the air. The air coordinator and the squadron leader then began questioning each torpedo-bomber pilot in turn: "249, did you drop?" The first pilot answered, "249, affirmative!" I was typing furiously, as I heard the next question: "221, did you drop?" The answer: "221, yes I dropped!" After one or two more "affirmatives," the next three or four began answering, "321, negative, did not drop!" "309, did not drop!"

The paper feed-out from my typewriter was requested immediately, as well as that of the other operator on the same radio channel. These would be checked over by investigators to determine what went wrong and why.

I don't recall the exact figures reported to us, but there were several casualties among the Seabees, including at least two or three who were killed. We in air support felt terrible about this. We blamed ourselves for allowing an inexperienced squadron to engage in close air support. For the remainder of this battle, the final one of World War II, we admitted only scheduled air strikes by Marine squadrons, or by Navy squadrons we knew had the expertise.

This was one of the many accidents which, because of wartime censorship, were never reported to the American public at the time, either by radio or in newspapers. In the context of total war, I believe censorship was a necessary thing. In this book, I have related other happenings, such as our casualty counts, underwater demolition teams, the tragic LST explosions in Pearl Harbor; and weapons like napalm and flame throwers. All such information was kept from the American public and from the enemy. Censorship was intended both to keep the enemy from learning things to his advantage, and to not demoralize the American public with alarming news of such devastating tactics as the enemy's *kamikazes* or our napalm.

Since World War II, we have engaged in several limited wars or quick engagements during the latter part of this century. Nowadays, an incident like dropping bombs on that Seabee camp is called, "friendly fire." Unfortunately, such gory scenes of death and destruction are now shown instantly, in graphic color to the public around the world by means of television videotaping and satellite communications. How ironic, that today's sensational media finds a way to twist the words describing such a tragic accident.

Five years after Okinawa, the First Marine Division, in Korea, allowed only Marine pilots to provide close air support to its troops on the ground.

That policy continues in effect to this day with the concept of Marine Air-Ground Teams. They train together and go into action together.

Okinawa
June 15, 1945

Dear Mother:

I would not expect to get home in time for any summer activities after this battle is over. Nine thousand miles is a long way, and we still have a lot of Japs to kill on this island before my outfit can shove off.

Waiting for a ship, here; stopping over, there; getting squared away at Ewa; waiting for a ship at Pearl Harbor; getting squared away on the West Coast; it will all take time.

I will look up Captain Kraker on the way back if our ship makes a stop at his island. It sounds as if he may be on Guam. I would have more reason to look him up than Admiral Furlong. You've introduced me to so many high-ranking Navy officers that I hardly know one from the other, except for Captain Schyler, or is he an admiral now?

The other day I spent some time up at the front lines and went through Naha. That once proud city of 65,000 people, capital of the Ryukus, is a heap of rubble. It is populated now, not by natives, but thousands of Marines. I had a vague idea that some of the houses would be worth living in, as we did in Charan Kanoa, back on Saipan. But there aren't many. The men pitch tents and tarps on sites where bulldozers have cleared away the ruins.
All the houses are behind high walls; and in some areas, walls are the only things left standing.

Now we hear the enemy is ignoring our ultimatum.

---

*   *   *

> *Okinawa*
> *June 21, 1945*
>
> **Dear Mother:**
>   *You say you seem to be thinking entirely about my getting home. Well, I am also. You should go easy on the anticipation or you'll get another bloating spell. That can become serious.*

Late in the campaign, the Navy wanted two small islets near Okinawa, Ibeya and Aguni, to be captured for radar installations. The 2nd Marine Division's 8th Regiment was ordered to come back from its base on Saipan to do the job. On June 3 the reinforced regiment landed, found little Japanese resistance, and declared the islands secured within twenty-four hours.

The 8th Marines were then ordered into the fighting on Okinawa. They were brought ashore on June 15 and assigned the task of spearheading an attack against the last remaining pocket of Japanese defenders. On June 17, Tenth Army General Simon Bolivar Buckner sent an offer of surrender to the enemy in the form of leaflets dropped by air. However, the Japanese commander, Lt. General Mitsuru Ushijima, rejected the offer.

General Buckner, shown here in front, was on hand shortly after noon

on June 18, 1945, to observe the fresh troops going into action in the valley below. As the Marines advanced across the valley, the Japanese defenders apparently noticed the unusual activity at our regimental observation post overlooking the scene. The enemy unleashed an artillery barrage against the hillside, which wounded several of our officers and men. Most notably, General Buckner was struck in the chest and died within ten minutes. He was the highest ranked American officer killed in action in World War Two, either in the European Theater of Operations or in the Pacific.

Commander of the Third Amphibious Corps, Major General Roy S. Geiger, the next-highest ranking American officer on the island, thus assumed command of the Tenth Army. Thereby, he became the

only Marine officer ever to have commanded a field army.

Shown here, left to right:

Gen. Geiger, Adm. Spruance, Gen. H. M. Smith, Adm. Nimitz, and Marine Corps Commandant, Gen. Vandergrift. Guam, 1944

Even though General Ushijima refused to make a formal surrender, apparently the news of our offer had spread through the remaining

From left: Maj. Gen. Roy S. Geiger, commander of III Amphibious Corps, Adm. Spruance, Lt. Gen. Holland Smith, Adm. Nimitz, and Lt. Gen. Alexander A Vandegrift, the Marine Corps commandant, meet at Geiger's headquarters on Guam in August 1944.

Japanese ranks, for, in the next few days, an unprecedented number of enemy troops did surrender. In all, 7,400 enemy soldiers surrendered during the three months of fighting, including about 1,000 wounded. This was the largest number of enemy prisoners taken in battle during the three-year offensive war in the Pacific.

General Geiger declared that Okinawa was secured on June 21, 1945. The next day, Lieutenant General Mitsuru Ushijima went to a high ledge overlooking the sea at the southern end of the island and committed hara-kiri.

Okinawa was the last island battle in the Pacific, and the bloodiest. About 130,000 enemy combatants were killed. More than 12,000 Americans died in action, including men of the three branches of service, almost equally divided among Army, Navy, and Marines. The Navy's total casualties, 9,731 dead and wounded, exceeded those of all the other Central Pacific island battles combined. Thirty-six American warships were sunk, and 368 others were damaged, mostly by *kamikazes*.

Twenty-seven years later, in May 1972, the United States returned Okinawa to Japan. Most of the 7,500 bodies of soldiers and Marines killed in action on Okinawa were removed to the "Punch Bowl" National Memorial Cemetery of the Pacific at Honolulu, Hawaii. Some, at family request, were sent back home for reburial in the contiguous forty-eight states.

HEADQUARTERS

MARINE AIR SUPPORT CONTROL UNITS,
AMPHIBIOUS FORCES, PACIFIC FLEET,
C/O FLEET POST OFFICE
SAN FRANCISCO, CALIFORNIA

The Commanding Officer takes pleasure in COMMENDING

Staff Sergeant Francis V. Gardner, USMCR,
for services as set forth in the following

CITATION

"For excellent service in the line of his profession in connection with the operation of Marine Landing Force, Air Support Control Unit One during the assault and occupation of both Iwo Jima and Okinawa. In both operations against the enemy, Staff Sergeant Francis V. Gardner, (481357), USMCR, under difficult conditions, performed his duties in a highly satisfactory manner. His devotion to duty, technical skill, and resourcefulness during the critical phases of the Iwo Jima and Okinawa campaigns contributed materially to the successful operation of Marine Landing Force, Air Support Control Unit One. His conduct under combat conditions was in keeping with the highest traditions of the Naval Service."

/signed/ Vernon E. Megee, Colonel, USMC, Commanding

Marine Landing Force, Air Support Control Unit One
Awarded the Navy Unit Commendation for action on Iwo Jima—

Vernon E. Megee	Colonel	Commanding officer

Following are forty-eight of the enlisted men from AWS-5, who survived the Battle of Saipan in 1944. Later, after being reorganized into the new LFASCU One under the command of Colonel Megee, we fought on both Iwo Jima and Okinawa in 1945.

John M. Bartley	Corporal	Radio operator
Daniel F. Bohleber	Sergeant	Power supply mechanic
Albert L. Buff	Technical sergeant	Radio operator
John Cangelosi	Private, first class	Radio operator
Angelo J. Cannizzaro	Corporal	Radio operator
Euclid K. Chappel	First sergeant	
John F. Church, USNR:	Pharmacist's mate, 1st Class	Medical corpsman
Randal D. Croley	Sergeant	Radio repairman
John E. Everette	Private, first class	General duty
Calvin W. Fahr	Private, first class	Radio operator
Francis V. (Frank) Gardner	Staff sergeant	Radio operator
William C. Herrman	Sergeant	Radio operator
William L. Holm	Sergeant	Radio repairman
Stanley F. Kochan	Sergeant	Power supply mechanic
George Konchar	Technical sergeant	Carpenter
John S. Kubalak	Staff sergeant	Administrative clerk
Robert Joseph	Technical sergeant	Radio mechanic
Edmund B. Liddle	Private, first class	General duty
James T. Linville	Corporal	Radio operator
Herman J. Mastrogiovanni	Sergeant	Radio operator
Francesco G. Merle	Private, first class	Automobile mechanic
Walter F. Michel	Sergeant	Radio repairman
Robert J. Moore	Staff sergeant	Radio operator
Joseph P. McGowan	Private, first class	General duty

Wilfred J. Nadeau	Sergeant	Radio operator
Johnnie F. Peek	Corporal	Radio operator
John C. Penney	Corporal	Radio operator
Gardner W. Pierce	Private, first class	Radio operator
Lawrence N. Pinto	Private, first class	Plotter, air warning
William H. Polk	Corporal	Radio operator
Samuel J. Ranallo	Corporal	Radio operator
Ernest R. Roberts	Sergeant	Radio operator
Andrew J. Samuelson	Sergeant	Plotter, air warning
Lawrence K. Schuster	Staff sergeant	Radio installation and repair
Melvin W. Shapiro	Sergeant	Plotter, air warning
Donald K. Soderholm	Technical sergeant	Radio operator
William Staats	Sergeant	Radio operator
Clyde A. Sullivan	Private, first class	General duty
Conrad N. Tallon	Corporal	Telephone man
Robert E. Thompson	Sergeant	Radio operator
Earl T. Trompeter	Corporal	Radio operator
Milton L. Urban	Sergeant	Radio operator
Milan Vujaklya	Sergeant	Property non-commissioned officer
Frank W. Watson	Cook	
Willard K. Webster	Master technical sergeant	Communications chief
Bernard K. White	Corporal	Radio operator
Robert W. Whittaker	Staff sergeant	Automobile mechanic
George A. Izquierdo	Sergeant	General duty

*   *   *

In the three battles we fought—Saipan, Iwo Jima, and Okinawa—only two men were killed, on Saipan under AWS-5:

Second Lieutenant Glenn A. Phillips, USMCR, was killed in action on Saipan at 11:30 a.m., June 29, 1944. He was buried July 1, 1944, in the 4th Marine Division Cemetery, Grave # 733.

Corporal Eugene P. Meacci, USMCR, was killed in action on Saipan June 29, 1944. He was buried June 30, 1944, in the Army Cemetery, Grave # 233.

Marine Corps records show that their personal effects were forwarded to USMC Effects Bureau, Clearfield, Utah.

Colonel Megee was our commanding officer from November 1944 through June 1945. He enlisted in the Marine Corps in 1919 and was commissioned a second lieutenant three years later. In the 1930s he took flight training and became a fighter pilot. Prior to World War II, he commanded a Marine fighter squadron.

For the outstanding performance as commander of our unit in close-air support, he was awarded the Legion of Merit with Combat" V" for Iwo Jima, and the Bronze Star with Combat "V" for Okinawa.

He remained in the Corps after the war and became a general officer. At the time of his retirement in 1958, he was in command of the Fleet Marine Force, Pacific. He was the first of only about two or three Marines ever to advance through the ranks from private to four-star general. General Megee died in January 1992 at the age of 91.

GEN VERNON E. MEGEE, USMC (RET.)

No Other Landing Force

They called us Landing Force, Air Support
  Control Unit One:
Marines who knew the difference 'tween
  A rifle and a gun.

We specialized in radio,
  Some radar business too.
To dig ourselves in better,
  Had our own construction crew.

At Miramar we trained,
  And went ashore at Coronado,
To practice hitting beaches
  Where United States Marines go.

From there, eight score of us
  Proceeded west by ocean trips,
To land on far off islands
  From nine oceangoing ships.

We hit the beach at Saipan,
  'Twas our first encounter then,
And in that bitter holocaust
  We lost some of our men.

We gave air warning to our troops,
  As fighting raged around.
We shed our blood, we mourned our dead,
  Amid the battle sound.

In four weeks it was victory
  And we were first to leave,
With fifteen hundred prisoners
  Oahu would receive.

Because the need for "quick air warning"
  Now was overcome,
Four dozen of us went to
  "Air Support," as "Unit One."

Yes, we were Landing Force, Air Support
  Control Unit One,
Restructuring at Ewa while
  We had a bit of fun.

The next place we assaulted
  Was for "aviation" sake,
Where three Marine divisions had
  Those three airfields to take.

'Twas living hell on Iwo Jima's
  Black, volcanic sand;
But 'ere that battle finished
  We received a new command.

We joined a huge armada
  That was headed westerly:
Twelve hundred ships, the greatest
  Ocean fleet in history.

On Okinawa we were met with
  Hide-and-seeker tactics,
As Navy guns were shooting down
  Young *"Divine Wind"* fanatics.

While *kamikazes* struck our fleet,
  And sunk three dozen ships,
We "grunts" ashore were searching out
  One hundred thousand Nips.

The slaughter lasted eighty days,
  And . . . would you still believe:
The forty eight of Unit One,
  Among the first to leave?

We made it home for Christmas, yes,
  For all we had been through.
To say our unit was unique,
  I don't mind telling you.

So, what's the point in all of this?
  What's all this telling for?
Well, those three island victories
  Were greatest of the war.

Not any other landing force
  Could claim what we had done:
Hit Saipan, Iwo, Okinawa.
  We, the only one.

Frank Gardner, July 1985

Note: Among the American combat units which assaulted Saipan, Iwo Jima, and Okinawa, including some two hundred thousand troops, only four-dozen Marines of our close air support unit fought in each of those, arguably, three toughest Pacific island victories of World War II.

Vow on Okinawa

One starry night on Okinawa, guns and men were still.
    This young Marine was standing duty on a lonely hill.
The battle ever carries on . . . two months it's been by now.
    All dead exceeding ninety thousand; and he wondered how.

How all the slaughter could continue under God's domain?
    How long are minds of men expected to endure the pain.
First Saipan . . . Iwo Jima next, he'd seen his buddies fall.
    And now, again on Okinawa . . . no letup at all.

And was there any reason why 'twas them instead of him?
    Perhaps a reason, somewhat subtle . . . more than just a whim.
On that occasion, then, he wondered why he felt so odd.
    He had a realization . . . as he felt the hand of God.

A pact was made that night in June of nineteen forty-five:
    A vow to God by that Marine . . . if he got home alive.
He'd make a contribution felt among his fellow man.
    He'd work to serve his country well, according to God's plan.

It's forty years now, since his vow was made that night in June.
    From his career in Government, he will retire soon.
His family, friends, and colleagues are the ones to tell us how . . .
    He made his contribution . . . and . . . how well he kept his vow.

Frank Gardner

Written in June 1985, the year
before the writer retired as a
Foreign Service Officer

CHAPTER 16

*   *   *

End of the War

Two weeks after the battle ended on Okinawa, LFASCU One, again was among the first troops to depart a captured island. On July 4, 1945, we boarded the *USS Rawlins*, APA 226, in Buckner Bay on the western side of Okinawa, across the island from where we had landed three months before. The name of the bay had been changed from Chimu to Buckner in honor of the Tenth Army's commanding general, who had been killed in action three weeks earlier. We weighed anchor on July 8th and sailed southeast.

Meanwhile, back home in Washington, my sister, Mary, followed my earlier suggestion about flowers for mother. She arranged with Gude Brothers Florist, 1124 Connecticut Avenue, for a vase of flowers to be delivered to mother on her birthday, July 11 at her office in the Navy Department, Room 4341, 17th and Constitution Avenue, 4th Floor, 3rd Wing.

Four days after departing Okinawa, we dropped anchor off Saipan, but did not go ashore. The next day we continued going southeast across the Central Pacific. The three previous crossings of the vast 3500-mile ocean between Hawaii and Saipan had taken an average of two weeks. Each of those times we had stopped for two or three days at Eniwetok.

This time we did not stop. We merely sighted Eniwetok and adjusted our course to northeast. Our crossing of that open stretch of ocean, therefore, took only nine days this final time.

We docked at Pearl Harbor on July 22, 1945, and returned to our home base at MCAS, Ewa. We moved into our barracks amid the curious stares of the main base personnel, many of whom had been spending most of the war in that relatively clean and orderly environment. Some of them, who knew we had just come from the far-off battlefront, looked on us with respect and admiration for what we had been through, much like the reception we had gotten the year before after returning from Saipan. Others, quite unaware of why our field uniforms may have appeared rather unkempt and worn, looked on us with some disdain.

Also, in mid-1945, when we returned to Ewa the final time, there was a new dimension to make us stand out from the main-base personnel. I recall occasions, usually in the base mess hall, when some freshly scrubbed young Marine, in neatly pressed uniform would approach a few of us. Out of curiosity, he'd make some amateurish inquiry as to why our skin was so yellow. We, of course, would point out that it was caused by Atabrine, which we had taken in the far Pacific islands to ward off malaria. We tried not to mention Okinawa to avoid more curious questions.

After we got settled in, I contacted LaVerne Cheely of main base personnel, who was taking care of Keynote in my absence. He informed me that Keynote had become so bonded with him over the long six-month period of my absence that he could not bear to give her back to me. I sent a delegation from my barracks to his barracks to negotiate a test for rightful ownership of Keynote.

It was agreed that Keynote would be stationed by handlers in the center of his barracks building, which was about 150 feet long, with bunks on either side and a door at either end. Cheely would appear at one door and I at the other. Whichever person Keynote went to would be declared the rightful owner.

The next day at the appointed time, Cheely's barracks mates, my friends, and some neutral observers all crowded into his building for the test. When I got to my assigned doorway, I could see Keynote being held by handlers in the center of the building, and Cheely, standing in the doorway at the other end of the barracks. At the signal to start, I did nothing, allowing him to make the first move. He immediately began calling Keynote by name and motioning for her to run to him. Her handlers let her go, and she began moving slowly toward where he was located at the far end of the building, her head and tail held down in a rather submissive attitude.

When she had covered half of the distance toward that end of the barracks, I whistled loudly the six-note tune I had taught her on Saipan: C D C B C, and high C. She stopped in her tracks and cocked one ear in the air. I whistled it again! She turned immediately and bolted back toward my direction, with her head held high and her tail wagging. She jumped up into my arms and greeted me amid the cheering of all the Marines in the place. There was no contest. I was awarded custody of Keynote by acclamation of all those present, including Cheely.

(Written at MCAS EWA)

July 24, 1945

Dear Mother:

I just heard from Hal again. Remember? The last time was back in January. He says he's doing fine. He expects to be where he is about a month or so and then move on. ("Hal" was in our "whereabouts code" for Hawaii. See letter dated, January 25, 1944.)

Keynote is doing fine. She's back with us now.

I was glad to hear of your making inquiries as to my rooming when I get back. 612 is out for me. (612 was the number of mother's one-room apartment at 1020 19th Street, N. W., in Washington)

> *Perhaps I could go back to the small room I rented in 1942 with Mrs. Meyers at 22 T Street, Northwest. I had a very good setup there. The room was very reasonable, and that appeals to me more than bunking in with someone else or living with family friends. I would like to have some peace, quiet, and solitude.*
>
> *I had thought of contacting Captain Kraker on the way back, but we did not stop very near his island.* (Guam) *At the one stop we made* (Saipan) *we weren't there long enough for me to get ashore and see Sister Angelica.*
>
> *Concerning Glen Carlyn, I think it's best to wait until I get back. After the war is over we can have a pow-wow about that.*

Again, as I had done the year before, I bought some more shoulder patches; first, was of the Third Amphibious Corps. I sewed it on my khaki shirts to show the outfit I had last been attached to in combat.

It is in the shape of a shield, showing an oriental dragon and a Roman numeral three on a field of red. Later on, in the fall, I sewed it onto the shoulder of my woolen forest green uniform jacket.

The other patch was of the Fifth Amphibious Corps. See next page.

The two Corps patches, along with the Second Marine Division patch, and Third Marine Wing patch are all displayed in a picture frame in my den at home. Also, I have medals from the war on display in a shadow box. They include medals for the American Campaign; World War II

Victory; and the Asiatic-Pacific Campaign, with three battle stars. Also in the shadow box are the sharpshooter medal I inherited from my father; my rifle expert medal; and my dog tag.

Shortly after arriving back at MCAS Ewa, we learned that we would be heading back to California to help form and train a new air-support-control unit. We hoped that we could fit in a furlough at home. After the new unit was formed and trained, we would all return to the Pacific in time for another invasion.

The Fifth Amphibious Corps patch, which I never had a chance to wear, is also in the shape of a shield, showing an attacking crocodile and three white stars on a field of red.

(Written at MCAS EWA)

July 27, 1945

Dear Mary:

I received mother's letter telling me about the flowers. I'm so glad she liked them. I too had thought about sending a little message on a card or something, but forgot about it in the shuffle, and the next thing I knew I was aboard ship. But everything came out all right.

Enclosed is $10.00 to take care of the bill. I didn't understand if the flowers alone were about $7, or if the vase was included. So, if this doesn't cover it, let me know.

Reading over one of your letters here, I see that you mention going into the convent in December. I feel sure I'll be home before then.

*   *   *

(Written at MCAS EWA)

> *July 29, 1945*
>
> *Dear Mother:*
> *I want to get off these money orders and send you back the two notes. I remember you asking for one of them.*
> *According to my records, these money orders bring up my savings to $400.00. I plan to send on more money later.*

*   *   *

(Written at MCAS EWA)

> *August 4, 1945*
>
> *Dear Mother:*
> *Yesterday I said good-bye to Keynote. After much internal debate for the past two weeks, I decided that she was a Marine dog and that the islands are where she belongs.*
> *In one of your back letters, you wondered how I spent July 4. Well, I spent the day boarding ship at Okinawa.*
> *Today I'm going into a transient camp for a few days before I board ship. Don't write anymore because I'm losing my mailing address now. You won't hear from me again until I get to the coast.*
> *I'll be home, at the earliest, in the last week of August. I'll be able to let you know more when I get to the States.*
> *I've lost much of the tan on my body, but not on my face. You'll have to judge for yourself about my Atabrine color.*
> *I hope it's cool enough to wear my* (woolen) *greens in the evening when I get back.*
> *I'll phone or wire you from the coast.*

I decided to have Cheely take care of Keynote again until I returned from the stateside tour. I realized that she was not as happy under his care as with mine. I could tell by her body language around him; but I didn't have enough time to search out a new custodian. He agreed to hold her for me until I got back from the States, with no further testing for rightful ownership. As things turned out, I never returned to Hawaii, so I never saw her again.

On August 6, 1945, a B-29 Superfortress, named *Enola Gay*, flew north from Tinian and dropped a uranium atomic bomb over the city of Hiroshima, Japan. Three days later, another B-29, named *Bock's Car (or Bockscar)* dropped a plutonium atomic bomb over the city of Nagasaki.

We learned about this while we were in a transient camp, waiting to board ship. The Honolulu radio and newspapers reported that the bombs were new weapons that caused great damage, the full extent of which was not known at the time. We figured that thousands were killed in both cities, but it would be months later that we would learn about the 70,000 killed in Hiroshima, and half that number in Nagasaki.

Two or three days later we boarded the *USS Copahee,* a small, escort aircraft carrier, numbered CVE 12. On August 13, we weighed anchor in Pearl Harbor and headed east, back to the United States. We expected to be back within about four months for an invasion of Japan. We would learn later that we would not have been in time for the first such landing on Kyushu; but we would make the second one on the main home island of Honshu, Japan, scheduled for early in 1946.

We were at sea one full day, when, on August 14, 1945, Japan announced its surrender, setting off wild public celebrations in the United States. It was called, "V-J Day," meaning, "Victory-over-Japan Day." Back on May 7, 1945, there had been similar celebrations when Germany surrendered. They were called, "V-E Day," meaning "Victory-in-Europe Day."

In the evening of that day, in August, we still had not heard the news. A few of us were gathered on the enclosed hangar deck of the *Copahee,* waiting for a movie to be shown. The ship's loudspeakers broke the silence with the usual three words, "Now hear this." Next, followed the simple, matter-of-fact announcement that the Japanese had surrendered. As we sat there on the rows of flat, wooden benches, hardly a word was spoken. I thought back to that moment on the hilltop on Okinawa and my prayer to God. We would not have to invade Japan. We could go home to live at peace with the rest of the world.

Just a few minutes later, another announcement came over the loudspeaker, informing us of the celebrations going on in the streets of San Francisco. Again, we were immersed in our own private thoughts. We talked quietly among ourselves about not having to fight a war anymore, about going home.

Years later I was interviewed about World War II by Reporter Alexandra B. Stoddard, whose article on Iwo Jima appeared in the February 19, 1991, issue of our local Potomac News. She asked me why we didn't celebrate there on that hangar deck, as the civilians had done in the United States. Miss Stoddard had focused in on my feelings. Her question took me unawares, and I didn't give a very good answer.

In this book, toward the end, I have admitted some of my feelings.

Why did we Marines not celebrate on board the *Copahee* that 14th day of August, fifty-three years ago? Perhaps, it was because no one started it. Apparently, there was no such spark among any of us to touch off an outward demonstration. We had all been through so much. We were psychologically prepared for action against the enemy, knowing we still had to invade Japan. Now, everything ended so quickly, so unexpectedly. We were speechless, immersed in our own thoughts.

We would not have to fight in combat any more, to be wounded any more, or die any more. We, as warriors, had not been programmed for any alternative other than war. We were not exuberant individuals, prone to independent self-expression. We were United States Marines who had learned how to fight a war, and now we would have to learn how to be at peace. Now, I can admit that I was quietly thanking God that I was going home alive. I suspect my other Marines were doing the same.

We arrived back in the United States on August 20, 1945, where our ship docked at Treasure Island in the middle of San Francisco Bay.

The war was over. A "point" system went into effect for discharge of military reservists. We were credited with points based on years of service, time overseas, and battle experience. Therefore, all of us in LFASCU One were in line for immediate separation from the armed forces. So, within two months, on October 18, 1945, I received my honorable discharge from the United States Marine Corps at Cherry Point, North Carolina. It is shown, front and back, on the next two pages:

Series 1

A415797

Honorable Discharge

SEMPER FIDELIS

FIDELI CERTA MERCES

United States Marine Corps

This is to certify that

Francis Victor GARDNER   a   Staff Sergeant

is Honorably Discharged from the Marine Wing Service Squadron Nine, 9th MAW, TNP. *and from the United States Marine Corps*

USMCAS, Cherry Point, N. C.

Reserve   this   18th   day of   October, 1945.

L. A. WREN.
Lieutenant Colonel, U.S.M.C.

This certificate is awarded as a Testimonial of Fidelity and Obedience.

Paid $100.00 Mustering Out Pay
this 18th day of October, 1945.
L. A. WREN.
Lieutenant Colonel, U.S.M.C.

Enlisted at RS, Washington, D. C. *on the* 30th *day of* September, 1942 *to serve* Dur. N. E. *years*

Born 2 December, 1922, *at* Washington, D. C.
When enlisted was 69½ *inches high, with* Blue *eyes;* Lt. Brown *hair,*
complexion: Ruddy *citizenship* U. S.
Previous service: None.

Rank and type of warrant at time of discharge: Staff Sergeant - Aviation Temporary.
Weapons qualification: Rifle Expert - score of 310. 2 September, 1944.

Special military qualifications: Radio Operator - SSN 776.

Service (sea and foreign): Central Pacific Area from 29 March, 1944 to 19 August, 1945.

Wounds received in service: None.
Battles, engagements, skirmishes, expeditions: Participated in the Saipan Operations.
Participated in the Iwo Jima Campaign. Participated in the Okinawa Campaign.

Remarks: Authority for discharge Art. 3-15, MCM. Issued Certificate of Satisfactory
Service; issued 2 patches, khaki, honorable service; issued 2 patches, green,
honorable service; issued USMC honorable discharge button.
Character of service excellent.
Serial number 481357   JOHN A. SCHUPP, Major., U. S. M. C. R.

Is physically qualified for discharge. Requires neither treatment nor hospitalization.
I certify that this is the actual print of the right index finger of the man herein mentioned. U. S. N.
and Medical Officer.

Monthly rate of pay when discharged $100.80
I hereby certify that the within named man has been furnished travel allowance at the rate of
3 *cents per mile from* Cherry Point, N. C. *to* Washington,
and paid $ *in full to date of discharge.*

(Signature of man)   JOHN A. SCHUPP, Major., U. S. M. C. R.
Commanding Officer

I returned to Mount Saint Mary's College, Emmitsburg, Maryland, to resume my undergraduate studies, taking advantage of the new veterans-benefit law to pay my way. The law was called, "The G I Bill of Rights." After two years, in 1948, I graduated with a Bachelor's Degree in Social Science.

I joined the Federal Bureau of Investigation in May 1948 as
a Special Agent. Then, at the Cleveland FBI Office in 1950, I met
Stenographer Gerry Donahue and married her the next year.
We had a family of nine children. After thirty-five years,
I retired in 1986 as a Foreign Service Officer.

Frank and Gerry Gardner, surrounded by their family, at home in Lake Ridge, Virginia, December 1987. Included are sons-in-law, and eleven grandchildren. (Left to right, rear) Daniel Gardner; Nancy Gardner; Robert Deane; Ellen Gardner (Deane)—*her Breathe Fund is the recipient of the proceeds from this book*; Lance Corporal Thomas Gardner, USMC; Lorraine Gardner holding son, Derek; Karen Gardner Sheehan holding daughter, Kelly; Thomas Sheehan. (Center) Diane Gardner Bowers holding son, David; Gerry Donahue Gardner holding granddaughter, Kacey Deane; Frank V. Gardner; Rosemarie Gardner. (Front) Linda Bowers (Christiansen), Angela Bowers, Joshua Bowers, Joseph Bowers, Jason Deane, Jeannine McDonnell, Cailin McDonnell, Maureen Gardner McDonnell, Robert McDonnell *(In January 2010, sworn in as Virginia's 71st Governor).*

Since the photo was taken, six additional grandchildren have been born: Rachel McDonnell; twins Robert and Sean McDonnell; John F. Deane; Joseph Gardner; and Elizabeth Gardner. Additionally, seven great-grandchildren have been born since this family portrait and the publication of this book.

APPENDIX

SAILING AND LANDING LOG
of Staff Sergeant Frank Gardner

March 19, 1944: Aboard *USS WASP,* CV 18. Weighed anchor at North Island, San Diego, California. Departed the United States, sailing west.

Ship number one.

April 3: Docked at Pearl Harbor, Oahu, Territory of Hawaii. (T. H.) Went ashore to the Marine Corps Air Station at Ewa.

May 12: Aboard the *USS SHERIDAN*, PA 61, in Honolulu Harbor, Oahu, T. H. Sailed south to Maui, T. H. Took part in maneuvers and practice landings. Returned to Oahu and remained aboard ship in Pearl Harbor.

Ship number two.

June 1: On PA 61, weighed anchor and departed Oahu, sailing west.

June 8: Dropped anchor in Eniwetok Atoll for refueling.

June 11: Weighed anchor and departed Eniwetok, sailing west.

June 15, 1944: D-Day on Saipan. Dropped anchor and landed on D-Day-plus-1by LCVP on northern Red Beach, attached to the 2nd Marine Division.

July 28: Weighed anchor and departed Saipan aboard the *USS J. FRANKLIN BELL,* PA 16, guarding 500 Japanese prisoners of war, sailing east.

Ship number three.

August 1: Dropped anchor and refueled at Eniwetok.
August 3: Weighed anchor and departed Eniwetok, sailing east.
August 10: Docked at Pearl Harbor, T. H. Went ashore to MCAS, Ewa.
January 25, 1945: Departed Pearl Harbor aboard *USS THURSTON,* PA 77, sailing west.

Ship number four.

February 4: Dropped anchor and refueled at Eniwetok.
February 7: Weighed anchor and departed Eniwetok, sailing west.
February 11: Dropped anchor off Saipan. Took part in maneuvers off Tinian.
February 16: Weighed anchor and departed Saipan, sailing north.
February 19, 1945: D-Day on Iwo Jima. Transferred to LST-784 and went ashore on Iwo Jima on D Day-plus-3 in 5th Marine Division sector.

Ship number five.

March 15: Boarded LST-84 at the beach on Iwo Jima. Sailed south.

Ship number six.

March 19: Dropped anchor in Tanapag Harbor. Went ashore on Saipan.
March 27: Boarded *USS BLADEN,* APA 63, in Tanapag Harbor. Departed Saipan, sailing west.

Ship number seven.

April 1, 1945: "Love" Day on Okinawa. (Easter Sunday) Dropped anchor
    and landed on Love Day by LCM at 6th Marine Division beachhead.

July 8: Boarded *USS RAWLINS*, APA 226, in Buckner Bay. Departed
    Okinawa, sailing east.

Ship number eight.

July 12: Dropped anchor off Saipan.

July 13: Weighed anchor; departed Saipan, heading east.

July 16: Sighted Eniwetok. Did not stop; continued sailing east.

July 22: Docked at Pearl Harbor, T. H., and went ashore to MCAS, Ewa.

August 13: Boarded *USS COPAHEE,* CVE 12, escort aircraft carrier, in
    Pearl Harbor.

Departed Oahu, sailed east toward the U. S.

Ship number nine.

August 14: News of Japanese surrender was announced to all hands and
    troops aboard ship.

August 20, 1945: Arrived back in the United States of America. Docked
    at Treasure Island, California, in San Francisco Bay.

Statistical Data from Three Islands Where I Landed
(See key page 251)

(All in the Central Pacific Area)		Killed or missing	Wounded	Prisoners (POW)	Total Casualties

SAIPAN: June 15 to July 9, 1944: Amphibious assault by 2nd & 4th Marine Divisions. Subsequent landing by Army's 27th Infantry Division D-Plus-2, June 17, 1944.

		Killed or missing	Wounded	Prisoners (POW)	Total Casualties
Marines:	Third costliest battle in Corps history	2,600 *	10,334 #	None	12,934 #
Army:	2nd costliest of Central or South Pacific Theaters	1,059 *	2,532	None	3,591 #
Navy:	4th costliest in support of Pacific island campaign	217 *	333 *	None	550
Total U. S. Forces:	Third costliest island victory	3,876	13,199	None	17,075
Enemy Forces:	Second costliest island battle	27,928 (POW)	236 (No wounds)	1,498 +&	29,662

Saipan: Third island-captured victory in total casualties on both sides: *46,737*

IWO JIMA: February 19 to March 26, 1945: Amphibious assault by the 4th and 5th Marine Divisions. Subsequent landing by the 3rd Marine Division D-Plus-5, February 24, 1945.

		Killed or missing	Wounded	Prisoners (POW)	Total Casualties
Marines:	Costliest battle in Corps history	6,126 $&	17,801 $&	None	$ 26,575
			(Combat fatigue: 2,648)		

(Statistics include 195 Navy corpsmen killed and 529 wounded with Marines on Iwo.)

(All in the Central Pacific Area)		Killed or missing	Wounded	Prisoners (POW)	Total Casualties
Navy:	3rd costliest in support of Pacific island campaign	686 $&	1,388 $&	None	2,074
Army:	Sixteen support units,	53 $++	116 $++	None	($++) 169

including the 471st, 473rd, 476th Amphibian Truck Companies (DUKW) and the 604th Graves Registration Company. Beginning D-Plus-7, February 26, the Army sent in three fighter squadrons. On D-Plus-18, March 9, 1945, the Army's 147th Infantry Regiment landed for garrison duty.

(Includes 44 air crewmen killed, 88 wounded, while sleeping, March 26, last day of battle.)

Total U. S. Forces:	2nd costliest island victory	6,865	21,953	None	28,818
Enemy Forces:	Fourth costliest island battle	21,784 ++	34 (POW)	182++&& (No wounds)	(++) 22,000

Iwo Jima: Second island-captured victory in total casualties on both sides   *50,818*

OKINAWA: April 1 to June 21, 1945: Amphibious assaults by the 1st and 6th MarDivs and the Army's 7th and 96th Infantry Divisions.

The Army's 27th Infantry Division went into action on Okinawa April 9; the 77th Infantry Division on May 1, 1945.

(All in the Central Pacific Area)		Killed or missing	Wounded	Prisoners (POW)	Total Casualties
Army:	Costliest island-captured victory	4,417 *	17,033 **	None	21,450
Marines:	2nd costliest battle in Corps history	3,112 *	13,523 **	None	16,635
Navy:	Costliest in support of Pacific island campaign	4,907 *#**	4,824 *#**	None	9,731
Total U. S. Forces:	Most costly victory in the Pacific	12,436	35,380	None	47,816
Enemy:	Costliest island battle; includes civilian fighters, downed fliers	130,539 **	1,166 (POW)	6,235 ** (No wounds)	137,940

Okinawa: First island-captured victory in total casualties on both sides: *185,756*

Total casualties on both sides at Saipan, Iwo Jima, and Okinawa: *283,311*

Key

(*) *On to Westward*, Robert Sherrod

(**) *The Marines' War*, Fletcher Pratt

(+) *Coral and Brass*, Gen. Holland M. Smith

(++) *IWO JIMA; Legacy of Valor*, Bill D. Ross

(#) *A Special Valor*, Richard Wheeler

($) *Directory*, 5MARDIV Jan. 1, '94

(&) Experience of Frank V. Gardner

(&&) *Encyclopedia Americana*

*   *   *

Statement by Fleet Admiral Chester W. Nimitz, Commander in Chief of the
United States Pacific Fleet and Pacific Ocean Areas, on March 17, 1945:

The U. S. Marines, by their individual and collective courage, have
achieved a base which is as necessary to us in continuing forward
movement toward final victory as it was vital to the enemy in staving off
ultimate defeat.

With certain knowledge of the cost of an objective, which had to be
taken, the Fleet Marine Force, supported by ships of the Pacific Fleet and
by Army and Navy aircraft, fought the battle and won.

By their victory, the 3rd, 4th, and 5th Marine Divisions and other
units of the Amphibious Corps have made an accounting to their country
which only history will be able to value fully.

For the Americans who served on Iwo Island, uncommon valor was
a common virtue.

Statistical Data from Eight Other Principal Islands Assaulted by Marine Divisions (MarDivs)

	Killed or missing	U.S. wounded; Enemy POWs	U.S. Sub-totals	U.S. Totals	Enemy Totals

GUADALCANAL, Solomon Islands, South Pacific Area, 8-7-42 to 2-9-43

Amphibious assault by 1MarDiv, with perimeter defense to Dec. 1942.
Units of 2MarDiv landed in November; full division in battle January 1943.

	Killed or missing	U.S. wounded; Enemy POWs	U.S. Sub-totals	U.S. Totals	Enemy Totals
Marines	1,300 #	2,900 #	4,200		
Navy	1,573 #	833 #	2,406		
Army:	American Division, October 1942; 25th Infantry Division December 1942.				
	470	1,900 #	2,370		
U.S. Forces	3,343	5,633	8,976		
Enemy Forces	26,100 #	1,200 #	27,300		

BOUGAINVILLE, Solomon Islands, South Pacific Area, 11-1-43 to 12-27-43

Amphibious assault by the Third Marine Division

	Killed or missing	U.S. wounded; Enemy POWs	U.S. Sub-totals	U.S. Totals	Enemy Totals
Marines	423 #	1.418 #	1,841		
Army	70**#	223**#	293	(37th Inf. Div. Nov. 17)	
Navy	99 #	186	285		
U.S. Forces	592	1,827		2,419	
Enemy Forces	4,591**#	25 #	4,616		

BETIO, TARAWA ATOLL, Gilbert Islands, Central Pacific Area, November 20 to 23,1943

Amphibious assault by the Second Marine Division

	Killed or missing	U.S. wounded; Enemy POWs	U.S. Sub-totals	U.S. Totals	Enemy Totals
Marines	990 +	2,311 +	3,301		
Navy	100**	200**	300		
U.S. Forces	1,090	2,511	3,601		
Enemy Forces	4,690 #	163 +	4,853		

	Killed or missing	U.S. wounded; Enemy POWs	U.S. Sub-totals	U.S. Totals	Enemy Totals

NEW BRITAIN, Bismarck Archipelago, Southwest Pacific Area: 12-26-43 to 4-22-44
Amphibious assault and holding action by First Marine Division

Marines	310 #	1,083 #	1,393		
Navy	101 #	199 #	300 #		
U.S. Forces	411	1,272	1,693		
Enemy Forces	4,730 #	20 #	4,750		

ROI-NAMUR, Kwajalein Atoll, Central Pacific Area, January 31 to February 2, 1944.
Amphibious assault by the Fourth Marine Division

Marines	229 *	797 *	1,026		
Navy	23 *	42 *	65		
U.S. Forces	252	839	1,091		
Enemy Forces	3,742**	264**	4,006		

GUAM, Mariana Islands, Central Pacific Area, July 21 to August 20, 1944
Amphibious assault by 3MarDiv and 1st Marine Provisional Brigade.

Marines	1,484 *	4,957 *	6,441		
Army	591 *	2,818 *	3,409 *	(77th Infantry Div. July 22)	
Navy	100 #	145 #	245 #		
U.S. Forces	2,175	7,920	10,095		
Enemy Forces	18,181 #	293 #	18,474		

	Killed or missing	U.S. wounded; Enemy POWs	U.S. Sub-totals	U.S. Totals	Enemy Totals

TINIAN, Mariana Islands, Central Pacific Area, July 24 to August 1, 1944
    Amphibious assault by 4MarDiv, followed by 2MarDiv on July 25.

Marines	431*#	1,735 *	2,166		
Navy	92 #	173 #	265 #		
U.S. Forces	486	1,879	2,331		
Enemy Forces	8,856 #	252 #	9,108		

PELELIU, Palau Islands, Central Pacific Area, September 15 to November 24, 1944
    Amphibious assault by 1MarDiv September 15 to October 15, 1944
    (This landing was designated L-Day, but the Marines called it, "Hell Day.")

Marines	1,241*#	5,024 #	6,265		
Army	277 #	1,008	1,285	(321st Inf. Reg. Sept. 23)	
Navy	156 *	114 *	270 *		
U.S. Forces	1,674	6,146	7,820		
Enemy Forces	10,381 #	302 #	10,683		

	U. S.	Enemy
Eight-island totals:	*38,026*	*83,790*
Total eight-island casualties on both sides:		*121,816*

Key

* *On to Westward*, Robert Sherrod	** *The Marines' War*, Fletcher Pratt
+ *Coral and Brass*, Gen. Holland M. Smith	# *A Special Valor*, Richard Wheeler

In 1942 and 1943, the three earliest Marine divisions invaded three main islands in the South and Southwest Pacific. In late 1943 and throughout 1944, four Marine divisions invaded six main islands in the **Central Pacific Area**. In 1945, all six Marine divisions were involved in the two greatest amphibious battles of the war, these, also in the **Central Pacific**. The Third, Fourth, and Fifth Marine Divisions were on Iwo Jima. The First and Sixth Marine Divisions, on Okinawa, with the 2nd Marine Division playing a lesser role there.

1st Marine Division	Guadalcanal 1942 South Pacific	New Britain 1943 Southwest Pacific*		**Peleliu 1944 Central Pacific**	**Okinawa 1945 Central Pacific**

*Loaned by Admiral Nimitz to General MacArthur

2nd Marine Division	Guadalcanal 1942 South Pacific	**Tarawa 1943 Central Pacific**	**Saipan 1944 Central Pacific**	**Tinian 1944 Central Pacific**	**Okinawa 1945 Central Pacific**
3rd Marine Division		Bougainville 1943 South/SW Pacific		**Guam 1944 Central Pacific**	**Iwo Jima 1945 Central Pacific**
4th Marine Division		**Roi-Namur 1944 Central Pacific**	**Saipan 1944 Central Pacific**	**Tinian 1944 Central Pacific**	**Iwo Jima 1945 Central Pacific**
5th Marine Division					**Iwo Jima 1945 Central Pacific**
6th Marine Division	****(1st Marine Provisional Brigade, the division's forerunner, landed on Guam with two regiments: The 4th and 22nd Marines.)**			**Guam: 1944 Central Pac. **(Two regiments)**	**Okinawa 1945 Central Pacific (Complete division)**

(The author is a life member in each of the six Marine division associations.)

Five U. S. Army Divisions were used predominantly in the U. S. Navy's **Central Pacific Area**. They participated in five major battles in that 3500-mile-wide ocean region. Three of those divisions, the 7th, 77th, and 96th, were "loaned" by Admiral Nimitz to General MacArthur in 1944 for the invasion of Leyte in the Philippines. They reverted to U. S. Navy command as part of the Tenth Army in 1945 for the Battle of Okinawa.

7th Infantry Division	Attu 1943 North Pacific	**Kwajalein 1944 Central Pacific**		Leyte 1944 Philippines	**Okinawa 1945 Central Pacific**
27th Infantry Division	Gilbert and Marshall Islands (Landings by separate regiments) 1943 and 1944—Central Pacific		**Saipan 1944 Central Pacific**		**Okinawa 1945 Central Pacific**
77th Infantry Division			**Guam 1944 Central Pac.**	Leyte 1944 Philippines	**Okinawa 1945 Central Pacific**
81st Infantry Division				Angaur 1944 **Central Pacific**	(After Angaur, 81st Div.'s 321st Regiment assisted the 1st Marine Division, L+8 on **Peleliu**.)
96th Infantry Division				Leyte 1944 Philippines	**Okinawa 1945 Central Pacific**

Fourteen other U. S. Army divisions were under General Douglas MacArthur for the offensive in the Southwest Pacific Area, including The Philippines. These included: the Americal; 1st Cavalry; 11th Airborne; 6th; 24th; 25th; 30th; 31st; 32nd; 37th; 38th; 40th; 41st; and 43rd. Also, four Australian Divisions: the 5th, 7th, 9th, and 11th, were under MacArthur on New Guinea in 1943 and 1944. (The 1st Marine Division was under MacArthur's command in the Southwest Pacific at New Britain in 1943.) (The Americal and 25th Divisions had reinforced the Marines on Guadalcanal in the South Pacific in late1942.)

Marine Divisions on Iwo Jima, February 19 to March 26, 1945

4th Division	5th Division	3rd Division (Feb. 24)
23rd Marine Regiment (Infantry)	26th Marine Regiment	9th Marine Regiment
24th Marines	27th Marines	21st Marines (Feb. 21)
25th Marines	28th Marines	3rd Reg. (Not used on Iwo)
14th Marines (Artillery)	13th Marines	12th Marines
4th Division Headquarters Bn.	5th Div. Hq. Battalion	3rd Div. Hq. Bn.
4th Amphibious Tractor Battalion	5th Amphibious Tractor Bn.	(No Amtrac Bn. indicated)
4th Engineer Battalion	5th Engineer Bn.	3rd Engineer Bn.
4th Medical Battalion	5th Medical Battalion	3rd Medical Battalion
4th Motor Transport Battalion.	5th Mtr. Transport Bn.	3rd Mtr. Transport Bn.
4th Pioneer Battalion	5th Pioneer Bn.	3rd Pioneer Battalion
4th Service Battalion	5th Service Battalion	3rd Service Battalion
4th Tank Battalion	5th Tank Battalion	3rd Tank Battalion
1st Joint Assault Signal Co.*	5th JASCO	3rd JASCO
1st Rocket Detachment*	3rd Rocket Detachment	(No rocket detachment reported)
4th War Dog Platoon	6th War Dog Platoon*	3rd War Dog Platoon
Marine Observation Sqdn.	4 Marine Obs. Squadron	5 Marine Obs. Sqdn. 1*
JICPOA Intelligence Team	JICPOA Intell. Team	JICPOA Intell. Team
*(Fought also on Okinawa.)		

*　　*　　*

Marine Units attached to the
Fifth Amphibious Corps (VAC) on Iwo Jima

2nd Armored Amphibian Battalion

2nd Bomb Disposal Company

2nd Separate Engineer Battalion

2nd and 4th 155mm Howitzer Battalions.

8th Field Depot

Civil Affairs Section

Evacuation Hospital Number One

JICPOA Enemy Materiel and Salvage Platoon

JICPOA Intelligence Team

Marine Landing Force, Air Support Control Unit One (Served also
with IIIAC on Okinawa)

Medical Battalion

Medical Section

Signal Battalion

Marine Divisions on Okinawa, April 1 to June 21, 1945

1st Division	**6th Division**	**2nd Division****
Landed on Love Day	**Landed on Love Day**	**(Fake landing**
April 1, 1945	**April 1, 1945**	**on Love Day)**
1st Marine Regiment (Infantry)	4th Marines	2nd Marines
5th Marines	22nd Marines	6th Marines
7th Marines	29th Marines	**8th Regiment****(June 1945)
11th Marines (Artillery)	15th Marines	10th Marines
1st Division Headquarters Bn.	6th Div. Hq. Battalion	2nd Div. Hq. Bn.
1st Amphibious Tractor Battalion	6th Amphibious Tractor Bn.	2nd Amtrac Bn.
1st Engineer Battalion	6th Engineer Bn.	2nd Engineer Bn.
1st Joint Assault Signal Co.*	6th JASCO	2nd JASCO
1st Medical Battalion	6th Medical Battalion	2nd Medical Battalion
1st Motor Transport Bn.	6th Mtr. Transport Bn.	2nd Mtr. Transport Bn.
1st Pioneer Battalion	6th Pioneer Bn.	2nd Pioneer Battalion
1st Rocket Detachment*	6th Rocket Detachment	2nd Rocket Detachment
1st Service Battalion	6th Service Battalion	2nd Service Battalion
1st Tank Battalion	6th Tank Battalion	2nd Tank Battalion
1st War Dog Platoon	6th War Dog Platoon*	2nd War Dog Platoon
Marine Observation Sqdn.	1* Marine Obs. Squadron	6 Marine Obs. Sqdn. 2
JICPOA Intelligence Team	JICPOA Intelligence Team	JICPOA Intell. Team

**(After fake landing, the 2nd Marine Division retired to its base on Saipan. Then, in June, its 8th Regiment returned to Okinawa to participate in the battle on land.)

*(Fought also on Iwo Jima.)

*   *   *

Marine Landing Force,
Air Support Control Units Assigned on Okinawa

Tenth Army

LFASCU #3

Twenty-fourth Army Corps	*3rd Amphibious Corps (Marine)*
LFASCU #2	**LFASCU #1** (Fought also on Iwo Jima.)

(Information is not available as to other Marine units attached to the Third Amphibious Corps on Okinawa. They would have been similar basic battalions in support, as shown for the Fifth Amphibious Corps on Iwo Jima.)

The 1974 Encyclopedia Americana gave the following casualty figures for the two World Wars.

The casualties of military belligerents in **World War I**, as reported by the United States War Department in 1924 were, as follows:

Countries	Total forces	Killed & died	Wounded casualties	Prisoners & missing	Total casualties
Allied Powers:					
Russia	12,000,000	1,700,000	4,950,000	2,500,000	9,150,000
France	8,410,000	1,357,800	4,266,000	537,000	6,160,800
British Empire	8,904,467	908,371	2,090,212	191,652	3,190,235
Italy	5,615,000	650,000	947,000	600,000	2,197,000
United States	4,355,000	126,000	234,300	4,500	364,800
Seven Others	2,904,343	407,944	343,492	287,938	1,041,374
Total	42,188,810	5,152,115	12,831,004	4,121,090	22,104,209

Countries	Total forces	Killed & died	Wounded casualties	Prisoners & missing	Total casualties
Central Powers:					
Germany	11,000,000	1,773,700	4,216,058	1,152,800	7,142,558
Austria-Hungary	7,800,000	1,200,000	3,620,000	2,200,000	7,020,000
Turkey	2,850,000	325,000	400,000	250,000	975,000
Bulgaria	1,200,000	87,500	152,390	27,029	266,919
Total	22,850,000	3,386,200	8,388,448	3,629,829	15,404,477
Grand Totals	65,038,810	8,538,315	21,219,452	7,750,919	37,508,686

World War II Armed Forces casualty figures:

Peak strength is the greatest strength reached at any
one time during the war.
Total strength means the total number of personnel during
the entire war.

Allied Powers Axis Powers

Nation	Peak strength	Battle deaths	Nation	Peak strength	Battle deaths
China	5,000,000	2,200,000	Bulgaria	450,000	10,000
France	5,000,000	210,671	Finland	250,000	82,000
India	2,150,000	24,338	Germany	10,200,000	3,500,000
Poland	1,000,000	320,000	Hungary	350,000	140,000
USSR	12,500,000	7,500,000	Italy	3,750,000	77,494
U. Kingdom	5,120,000	244,723	Japan	6,095,000	1,219,000
United States	12,300,000	292,131	Rumania	600,000	300,000
10 Others	3,801,000	579,418			

United States Armed Forces total strength and casualties in World War II:

Service	Total strength	Battle deaths	Other deaths	Wounds	Captured or missing
Army	11,260,000	234,874	83,400	565,861	135,524
Navy	4,183,466	36,950	25,664	37,778	2,429
Marine Corps	669,100	19,733	4,778	67,207	1,756
Coast Guard	241,093	574	1,345	955	
Total	16,353,659	292,131	115,187	671,801	139,709

Total American Casualties in World War II: 1,218,828

*   *   *

During this twentieth century, the United States has fought in five wars around the world. For those readers who may need some gauge or measurement to understand the impact of those wars, one category alone will show how they compared. The Americans killed in action during World War II exceeded by 74,000 the number killed in the other four wars of this century combined:

Total Americans killed or died of wounds in World War II (1940s):   *292,131*

Total Americans killed or died of wounds in World War I (1918):   126,000

Total Americans killed or died of wounds in the Korean War (1950s):   33,629

Total Americans killed or missing in the Vietnam War (1960s & 70s):   58,175

Total Americans killed or missing in the liberation of Kuwait (1990)   52
(According to Pentagon figures in Potomac News, February 26, 1991):   _____
Total casualties in four other wars, combined   *217,856*

(All statistics, except in 1990, were taken from the 1974 Encyclopedia Americana.)

ADDENDUM

Five years after the war, while stationed in Cleveland, Ohio, as a Special Agent of the Federal Bureau of Investigation, I joined a local chapter of the Marine Corps Reserve early in 1950. Later that year, the Korean War broke out. On February 15, 1951, I was ordered to report for active duty in the Marine Corps at Camp Lejeune, North Carolina. On March 1, 1951, the order was cancelled "in view of your position with the Federal Bureau of Investigation."

Meanwhile, about that time all Marines were invited to contribute to the placement of a Marine Corps War Memorial beside Arlington Cemetery across the Potomac River from Washington, D. C. As I recall, I responded with a check in the amount of $25.00.

Among the 20-person Board of Directors were listed the following:

Colonel Jean W. Moreau, Foundation Secretary
Fleet Admiral Chester W. Nimitz, former Commander in Chief, Pacific Fleet
General Harry Schmidt, former commander, Marine Fifth Amphibious Corps
General Holland M. Smith, former commander, Fleet Marine Force
Colonel Ruth C. Streeter, commander of the Women Marines

Later, I received the following acknowledgment:

Marine Corps War Memorial Foundation
Henderson Hall
U. S. Marine Corps Headquarters
Washington, D. C.
4 April 1951

Dear Mr. Gardner:

You, as a Marine Reservist, have the sincere thanks of the entire Foundation and the Marine Corps as a whole for your generous contribution to the Marine Corps War Memorial Foundation, Inc.

You will be pleased to know the drive is well underway and we are expanding our solicitation step by step and hope to eventually launch a national drive to the public.

This Memorial will be a permanent and fitting tribute to all Marines past, present and future and to the generosity of people like you.

Again, thanks for your donation. Believe me when I say, it was sincerely appreciated.

Cordially,
J. W. Moreau
Col., USMC, Ret.
Foundation Secretary

The Memorial is dominated by a huge bronze sculpture, done by Felix de Weldon, patterned after the Pulitzer Prize-winning photograph of Associated Press Photographer Joe Rosenthal. It depicts five Marines and a Navy corpsman raising the American Flag atop Mount Suribachi on Iwo Jima, February 23, 1945.

Although it is dedicated to the memory of all Marines who have fought for this country since 1775, it seems that most people refer to that hallowed site as the Iwo Jima memorial or monument.

At the 50th Anniversary of the Battle of Iwo Jima in Washington, D.C., February 19, 1995, my daughter, Lorraine, and I met Felix de Weldon. We both secured his autograph. I placed my copy in my loose-leaf binder on World War II.

During the publishing process of this book, on June 19, 2010, Frank Gardner passed away peacefully, in his home, surrounded by his children and grandchildren. He went to join his bride, Gerry, of 58 years of marriage, who had passed away a year and two days prior, on June 17, 2009. This book was something that Frank was very proud of. He put a lot of effort into telling his story of a war that most certainly changed the face of this great nation and its people, including a young man named Frank. We (Frank's family) sincerely hope that you have enjoyed reading it. Semper Fi, Dad!

Signed,

Tom Gardner
(Frank's son, youngest of nine, on behalf of all)

The Marine Corps War Memorial, Arlington, Virginia

The Marines' Hymn

From the Halls of Montezuma
To the shores of Tripoli,
We fight our country's battles
In the air, on land, and sea.
First to fight for right and freedom,
And to keep our honor clean,
We are proud to claim the title
Of UNITED STATES MARINE.

Our flag's unfurled to every breeze
From dawn to setting sun;
We have fought in every clime and place
Where we could take a gun.
In the snows of far off northern lands
And in sunny tropic scenes,
You will find us always on the job:
The UNITED STATES MARINES.

Here's health to you and to our Corps
Which we are proud to serve;
In many a strife we've fought for life
And never lost our nerve.
If the Army or the Navy
Ever look on Heaven's scenes,
They will find the streets are guarded
By UNITED STATES MARINES.

BIBLIOGRAPHY

Battle at Iwo Jima, The: Commemorative Volume. Nashville: Turner Publishing, 1990.

Costello, John. *The Pacific War 1941 - 1945*. New York City: Harper Collins Publishers, 1982.

Dictionary of American Naval Fighting Ships. District of Columbia: Naval Historical Center, 1959.

Encyclopedia Americana. Danbury, Connecticut. Grolier, Inc., 1974.

Fahey, James C., Associate. *The Ships and Aircraft of the U.S. Fleet - War Edition.* Annapolis, Maryland: United States Naval Institute, 1942.

Ireland, Bernard, Eric Grove. *Jane's War at Sea 1897-1997: 100 Years of Jane's Fighting Ships*. London; Collins Reference, 1997

"Japanese Soldier, The." *The Infantry Journal.* District of Columbia, 1943.

Manchester, William. *Goodbye, Darkness*. New York City: Dell Publishing, 1987.

McMillan, Zerlinden, et al. *Uncommon Valor: Marine Divisions in Action.* Nashville: Battery Press, 1986.

Pratt, Fletcher. *The Marines' War.* New York City: William Sloan Associates, 1948.

Ross, Bill D.. *Iwo Jima: Legacy of Valor.* New York City: Vanguard Press, 1985.

Sherrod, Robert. *On to Westward.* New York City: Duell, Sloan, and Pearce, 1945.

Smith, Holland M., General, USMC,. *Coral and Brass.* New York City: C. Scribner's Sons, 1949.

Tatum, Charles W. *Iwo Jima: Red Blood – Black Sand.* Stockton, California: C.W. Tatum Publishing, 1995.

Wheeler, Richard. *A Special Valor.* New York City: Penguin Group (USA), Inc., 1985.

*   *   *

2MarDiv Association's *Follow Me* of Sept. 1994, p.18, 19, 25 and 26
4MarDiv Association's Newsletter of September 1994, page 20.
5MarDiv Association's Membership Directory, January 1, 1994, p. 5
6MarDiv Association's Newsletter of March 1994, p. 24, about P. Harbor
Scripps Howard News Service, reporting on 50 years ago in WWII
World War II Magazine, January 1995, p. 56 re air support on Iwo Jima

CPSIA information can be obtained at www.ICGtesting.com
Printed in the USA
LVOW07s2104010115

421097LV00001B/202/P